KATE QUINTON'S DAYS

Books by Susan Sheehan

Ten Vietnamese

A Welfare Mother

A Prison and a Prisoner

*Is There No Place
On Earth for Me?*

Kate Quinton's Days

SUSAN SHEEHAN

KATE

QUINTON'S

DAYS

HOUGHTON MIFFLIN COMPANY

BOSTON

1984

Library of Congress Cataloging in Publication Data

Sheehan, Susan.
Kate Quinton's days.

1. Quinton, Kate, 1902–   . 2. Aged — United States
— Biography.   3. Aged — Diseases — United States —
Biography.   I. Title.
HQ1064.U6N474   1984   305.2'6'0924   84–6660
ISBN 0–395–36220–2

Printed in the United States of America

v 10 9 8 7 6 5 4 3 2 1

For Brendan Gill,
and no wonder

· ACKNOWLEDGMENTS ·

I WISH TO EXPRESS my gratitude to those who so kindly
cooperated in the preparation of this book. Particular
thanks are due to Herbert Sturz, David Gould, and Diane
Confalone. I am also thankful to Susan Berresford of the
Ford Foundation, to Gregory Farrell of the Fund for
the City of New York, and to the Ford Foundation and the
Fund for the City of New York for their generous financial
assistance; to Suzanne E. Thorin and Bruce Martin of the
Research Facilities Office of the Library of Congress; to
Robert, Susan, and Susannah Lescher; and to Nan A.
Talese, Gail Ross, Clay Morgan, and Signe Warner of
Houghton Mifflin.

It is always a joy to acknowledge the help so many of
my colleagues at *The New Yorker* have given me: Laurie
Witkin; Ann Goldstein, Eleanor Gould, Elizabeth Macklin,
Susanne Leary Shoemaker, and Edward Stringham; Sheila
McGrath, John O'Brien, and Natasha Turi; Edith Agar,

Linda Plantz, and Helen Stark; Joseph R. Carroll, John
M. Murphy, Bernard J. McAteer, William J. Fitzgerald,
John Broderick, Patrick J. Keogh, and Victor Webb;
Bruce Diones, Luis Feliciano, Timothy Hoey, Ashley
Kahn, John Paribello, and Edwin Rosario; Anne Neglia
Caldarera, Patricia Goering, Rose Marano, and Robert
Gerin. I owe special thanks to William Shawn for his gift
of the title and to John Bennet and Patti Hagan for their
elegant editing and checking.

I continue to enjoy my visits with Kate and Claire Quinton, whose friendship has been the greatest reward of
this book.

◄§

The names of all the people mentioned in this book are
fictitious except as mentioned below, and, where necessary to disguise the identity of the central characters, de-
scriptive details have been altered. I have used the real
names of Herbert Sturz, George Adams, Howard Hornstein, David Gould, Diane Confalone, Cindy Strong,
Robert Speirs, and Rose Carrese.

KATE QUINTON'S DAYS

CHAPTER ONE

FEBRUARY 24, 1982, was a cold day in New York City. Kate Quinton, a pale, thin elderly woman, lay in a bed at Lutheran Medical Center in Brooklyn. The winter-gray afternoon light filtered into her room. Her throat was sore and her feet were swollen. She lay still. She occasionally glanced across the room at her closet (it was marked "A") and at her roommate's closet ("B"). She looked at A and then B, B and then A, as she had been doing for days. Then her eyes focused on the clock in the hall outside her room. It was four o'clock; three minutes past four; five minutes past four.

Mrs. Quinton had been admitted to Lutheran Medical Center on January 5, 1982. She had felt mild abdominal pain for several weeks before that. On New Year's Day, the pain had become more intense; it had been accompanied by nausea and vomiting. On the evening of January 5, Mrs. Quinton was sitting at the dinette table in the apartment she shared with her daughter Claire. She had had no appetite for days and had taken only a few bites of the dinner Claire had prepared. "I just can't get anything down," she said. She told Claire that the pain had become unbearable, and got up from her chair, carefully transferring her weight to a walker; she had been using the walker off and on for the past two years, because she had experienced several spells of faintness and because she had severe arthritis in her knees and feet. As she was walking slowly toward her bedroom, a sudden weakness overcame her in the hallway between the kitchen and the bedroom. She couldn't take another step. "I'm going to collapse," she told Claire. "Bring me a chair, quick."

As soon as Mrs. Quinton was seated, Claire went downstairs to get her landlord, Mario Rossi. The Quintons rented the second floor of a two-family house in the Windsor Terrace section of Brooklyn. Mr. Rossi lived with his family on the ground floor. Mr. Rossi came up immediately and carried Mrs. Quinton to her bed — something that Claire, who had had five spinal fusions and walked with a cane, was unable to do. Claire reflected that it was fortunate her mother hadn't put on her clothes that day; she was wearing a nightgown and a dressing gown. After Mr. Rossi left, Claire telephoned William Ruffolo, her mother's doctor. She described her mother's symptoms to Dr. Ruffolo — the increasing pain in the lower abdomen, the nausea, the dark-brown urine her mother had been passing. Dr. Ruffolo told Claire that he was just leaving his office to take care of a patient who had suffered a cardiac arrest. He couldn't come to see Mrs.

Quinton, and suggested that Claire telephone Doctors-on-Call, an agency based in Brooklyn that employs around two hundred physicians part time and full time who make hundreds of house calls a week — the house calls that most private doctors stopped making many years ago. Twenty-five minutes after Claire telephoned Doctors-on-Call, the Quintons' doorbell rang. Claire went downstairs and let in a boyish-looking physician, who identified himself as Dr. Edward Batzel. Dr. Batzel took Mrs. Quinton's blood pressure — it was normal — and said he was going to examine her. He pressed down on several parts of her abdomen. "Ouch! Ouch! Ouch!" Mrs. Quinton said. Dr. Batzel's examination ended with Mrs. Quinton's cries of pain. He advised Claire to call an ambulance and take her mother to the emergency room of the hospital of her choice. He recommended an ambulance company that usually responded promptly. Dr. Batzel gave Claire a bill for forty dollars and his Doctors-on-Call card. While she was writing out a check, he told her that he would be more than glad to take care of her mother again if she ever needed him. Claire Quinton telephoned the ambulance company, gave the dispatcher her name and address, and said that she wanted to go with her mother to Lutheran Medical Center, a 532-bed voluntary hospital in the Sunset Park section of southwest Brooklyn, about a ten-minute ride from the Quintons' apartment. Dr. Ruffolo had admitted Mrs. Quinton to Lutheran in June of 1981 after a lump was discovered in her right breast; the lump, which proved to be benign, had been removed there. The ambulance appeared within half an hour, as Claire was putting a box of baking soda (which her mother used to brush her dentures) and other sundries in a small suitcase. Two attendants lifted Mrs. Quinton onto a stretcher and carried her down the steep flight of stairs. The ambulance's shock absorbers were worn out. Claire winced as the vehicle bounced up and down along the potholed streets. At the hospital, she wrote out a check for ninety dollars to the ambulance company.

Lutheran's emergency room wasn't busy at 9 P.M. on January 5. While Mrs. Quinton was being examined by one of the nurses and one of the interns on duty, Claire stood at the emergency-room desk, where a clerk was seated at a computer terminal. The clerk asked her a lot of questions about her mother. The answers appeared on the "face sheet" of Mrs. Quinton's hospital chart. Date of birth: 2/11/02. Marital status: Widow. Place of birth: Scotland. Religion: Catholic. Place of worship: Immaculate Heart of Mary. Current occupation: Homemaker. Social Security number: Claire recited the nine digits from memory. Insurance carrier: Medicare. Policy number: It was the same as Mrs. Quinton's Social Security number, followed by the letter "D," for widow's benefit. (Though Mrs. Quinton had worked for three decades, she had had Social Security taxes deducted from her paychecks for only four years. She received Social Security benefits on her late husband's work record and used his Social Security number rather than her own.) Attending physician: Ruffolo. Name of relative to notify in case of emergency: Claire Quinton. Relative's work phone: None.

When the clerk was finished with Claire, she was allowed to go into the examination cubicle, where her mother was answering her share of questions. Mrs. Quinton told the nurse, the intern, and, presently, a resident that the mild abdominal pain she had first felt six weeks earlier had become unbearable in the last two or three days. As the hours went by in the emergency room, the account of her symptoms became a twice- and a thrice-told tale. She had lost her appetite and believed she had also lost weight in recent weeks; she guessed she weighed 115 pounds. The resident described her on the chart as "poorly nourished," which embarrassed Claire when a nurse later mentioned it to her. Mrs. Quinton said she used alcohol socially, and she owned up to having smoked a pack of cigarettes a day for thirty-four years. She said she considered herself in fair health except for her arthritis, which limited her activities and sometimes caused her to feel depressed. Her vital signs were good, her neurological reflexes were normal, and she was in no acute distress, but the young doctors who saw her had no doubt that she needed to be admitted to Lutheran. They called Dr. Ruffolo, and he instructed them to admit her. They gave her an "admitting" diagnosis of Urinary Tract Infection/Rule Out Renal Malignancy. Between 9 P.M. and 1 A.M., Mrs. Quinton spent most of her time in the cubicle. At one point, an electrocardiogram was done, and she was wheeled away for a chest X-ray and for an X-ray of her abdomen. The resident's plans for Mrs. Quinton included a complete blood count, a urinalysis, a liver scan, an intravenous pyelogram (the injection into the veins of a radio-opaque dye that the kidneys concentrate, so that they become visible on an X-ray film), and an abdominal-renal sonogram, which shows the outlines of the organs by means of sound waves. At one o'clock on the morning of January 6, Claire Quinton was told that her mother would be taken to a room and that she could no longer stay with her. No one in the emergency room knew which room. Mrs. Quinton was frightened. Claire was advised to call the hospital in the morning for her mother's room number and direct-dial telephone number. Claire Quinton had telephoned her sister, Barbara, who lived in Teaneck, New Jersey, at 9:30 P.M. from a pay phone near the emergency room. Barbara's husband, Dwight Gaylord, had answered the telephone. Claire had told Dwight that her mother was at Lutheran. Dwight had said that Barbara was already asleep. He hadn't offered to wake her. Claire called a car service from the same pay phone. Residents of southwest Brooklyn use private car services much more frequently than taxicabs, because taxicabs rarely cruise the streets in the area. She got home around 1:30 A.M.

A few hours later, Dr. William Ruffolo came to Lutheran. He found Mrs. Quinton in Room 5911. He read the intern's and the resident's descriptions of their examinations of Mrs. Quinton, the history they had taken of her present illness, her past medical history, and the resident's notes and initial plans for treatment. Dr. Ruffolo examined Mrs. Quinton and told her she would be in the hospital for a short while to have some tests. He added an Attending's Admission Note to her chart, in which he stated that he agreed with the history and the physical findings of the resident. His impression was that Mrs. Quinton had a urinary-tract infection; he wanted a genito-urinary malignancy ruled out. He also wanted to rule out hepatitis, gallbladder disease, and kidney disease. He concluded his note with "ELS — 1 wk, D/P — home"; that is, he estimated that Mrs. Quinton's length of stay at Lutheran would be one week and his plan was to discharge her to her home.

A renal sonogram done on January 7 showed that Mrs. Quinton's right kidney was normal; the radiologist couldn't judge her left kidney, because she was unable to lie prone. An abdominal sonogram taken that day showed no abnormality of the liver. Mrs. Quinton appeared to have some sludge within the gallbladder; thus, according to the radiologist, "gallstones cannot be excluded." The following day, an intravenous pyelogram was taken; it was not altogether clear, but what could be seen was "unremarkable." On January 12, a liver scan showed the liver and spleen to be normal. After Mrs. Quinton's first few days in the hospital, her catheter was draining amber urine, her I.V. was infusing well, and her abdominal pains had diminished. The urinary-tract infection had cleared up, but her appetite remained poor. To supplement the calories Mrs. Quinton was getting intravenously and on a soft diet, a nutritionist prescribed strawberry milkshakes. When Mrs. Quinton complained about the milkshakes, she was given the eggnogs she requested. She preferred soup Claire bought for her at a neighborhood delicatessen and brought to the hospital in a thermos on daily visits to either the milkshakes or the eggnogs. After seven days at Lutheran, Mrs. Quinton was lethargic and weak. She was scheduled for additional tests — another X-ray of the abdomen, a barium enema, an upper-gastrointestinal series. Dr. Ruffolo's original "ELS — 1 wk" had come and gone; his terse subsequent notes did not include an estimated length of stay. His original "D/P — home" had also apparently been amended. A note written by a resident on Mrs. Quinton's chart on January 13 read, "Pt. not too pleased about prospect of going to a nursing home." The previous afternoon, Mrs. Quinton had said little to Claire in five hours except "Get me out of here. Get me back where I belong. I'll get back on my feet at home." When Claire replied that she would have to be patient, her mother said, "Patience has never been one of my virtues." Claire told her mother that she might not be able to take her home directly from the hospital, whenever she was released, because she wouldn't be able to lift her or take proper care of her. Claire had told her mother that she might first have to go to a nursing home for four to six weeks to regain some of her strength.

꿍

Unbeknown to Claire, one of Mrs. Quinton's nurses was thinking along the same lines. On January 13, the nurse referred Mrs. Quinton to Lutheran's Social Service Department. The following day, Robert Speirs, a social-work assistant who was responsible for helping most of the medical and surgical patients on Lutheran's fifth floor with their post-hospital plans, reviewed Mrs. Quinton's chart and telephoned Claire. He introduced himself and asked Claire if she was considering nursing-home placement for her mother. When she said she was, he told her that nursing homes in New York City charged "private pay" patients about seventy-five dollars a day. Claire said that neither she nor her mother had that kind of money. Mr. Speirs told Claire that Medicare, with very few exceptions, did not pay for nursing-home care, but Medicaid did. (Medicare is a federal health-insurance program for the aged or disabled. Medicaid is a federal and state health-insurance program for people unable to afford medical care.) Speirs asked Claire what her mother's monthly income was. She said that it was $271.10 — Mrs. Quinton's monthly Social Security check. He asked her what her mother's liquid assets were. She said they were about $2500. In January of 1982, the monthly-income ceiling for Medicaid for a single person in New York State was $333.33. The ceiling on liquid assets, such as savings (homes and such personal property as furniture and one automobile were exempt from this ceiling), was $2500. Bob Speirs told Claire he believed that her mother was "Medicaid-eligible." He suggested that she have her mother apply for Medicaid as soon as possible, because Medicaid applications often took from three to four months to be processed. Claire said she would think it over.

Mrs. Quinton's second week at Lutheran was no less difficult than her first. Her arthritis was hurting her. She was having trouble keeping her food down. She didn't want to eat. She felt weaker. Barbara telephoned every day, and paid a daily charge of $3.82 so that her mother could have a small television set next to her bed, but Mrs. Quinton rarely watched TV. Her eyes were bothering her — she seemed to need new glasses — and she found most television programs boring. Although Claire came to the hospital each day at two-twenty and stayed until after seven, when the mail and the day-after-tomorrow's menus had been delivered, Mrs. Quinton asked the nurses why her other relatives, including Barbara, didn't come to see her. She was receiving fewer get-well cards and phone calls from her sisters and her friends than she would have liked. Her first roommate slept most of the day and never spoke; she appeared to be terminally ill. Mrs. Quinton was depressed by her roommate's situation and by her own. One morning, she told a nurse that she was going to see her lawyer about the care given at Lutheran. After Mrs. Quinton had had a week of bed rest, Sally Thurman, her "primary care" nurse, who was on the 7:15 A.M. to 3:30 P.M. shift, got her out of bed, tied her with a sheet into a chair with a tray rest, and left her there for three hours. Mrs. Quinton complained to Claire, who complained to Mrs. Thurman that her mother was left in the chair too long. Mrs. Thurman's reply was "Kate didn't come to the hospital with pneumonia, and she isn't going to get pneumonia at Lutheran, because I don't have time to take care of a pneumonia case."

On January 19, Claire called Barbara. She told her sister she thought their mother would have to go to a nursing home temporarily. "I'll support your decision fully," Barbara said. Barbara had a job selling cosmetics from nine until three. Her husband owned an air-conditioning sales-and-service company. Dwight Gaylord had turned fifty-five on December 30, when the Gaylords were out of town. Barbara said that she and Dwight would visit her mother at the hospital the following day after four. They would stay for two hours and would then take Claire out to dinner for a belated celebration of Dwight's birthday. Claire said she would go to the hospital early on the twentieth, leave before Barbara and Dwight arrived, and wait at home for them to pick her up.

On the morning of January 20, Claire telephoned Dr. Ruffolo. She told him what she had told her sister the previous evening about her mother's apparent need to spend a few weeks in a nursing home. She asked him to meet her at Lutheran that afternoon; she said she needed his moral support. He agreed, and offered to get in touch with Bob Speirs. When Dr. Ruffolo came to Kate Quinton's room that afternoon and spoke the words "nursing home," Mrs. Quinton told him and Claire that she had once seen a television show that exposed the horrible conditions in some nursing homes. Dr. Ruffolo assured her that there were some excellent nursing homes in Brooklyn, and that she would be in a nursing home for only a short period. "Kate, Claire is doing the right thing for both of you," he said. A few minutes after Claire had thanked Dr. Ruffolo for pacifying her mother and had walked with him to the door, Bob Speirs came to Mrs. Quinton's room. He spoke to her about several nursing homes, in Brooklyn and on Staten Island. He mentioned one on Staten Island that had particularly nice rooms, with beautiful views of the Manhattan skyline. Claire Quinton wasn't sure that her mother had heard everything Bob Speirs said — Mrs. Quinton is deaf in her right ear and misses parts of many conversations — but Claire didn't think her mother would care one way or the other about a room with a view. Claire was sure she didn't want her mother on Staten Island. The daily drives there over icy streets were more than she could handle in winter. When Bob Speirs brought up Mrs.

Quinton's finances, Claire suggested that they continue their discussion elsewhere. Mrs. Quinton had had gall-bladder X-rays that morning; she was tired and wanted to rest up for Barbara's eagerly awaited first visit.

In Bob Speirs's office, Claire Quinton said that her monthly income was a Social Security disability check for $472.40; she hadn't been able to work since 1976. Mr. Speirs told Claire that she wasn't applying for Medicaid, and that her income had no bearing on her mother's eligibility for Medicaid. He again said he believed that her mother was eligible. Claire said she would have her mother apply. Mr. Speirs telephoned Haydee Santana, a counselor in Lutheran's Patient Accounts Department, whose job it is to help people apply for Medicaid. He made an appointment for Claire to see Miss Santana the following day. He gave Claire a list of the documents she would need to show Miss Santana: her mother's birth certificate, marriage and citizenship papers; Mr. Quinton's death certificate; a Social Security card; some recent canceled rent and utility receipts; and her mother's bankbook or bankbooks. He also gave Claire a list of about twenty nursing homes in Brooklyn, Queens, and Staten Island. The names of four nursing homes in Brooklyn had check marks alongside them in the margin; these were nursing homes to which Lutheran's Social Service Department sent many of the hospital's patients. Claire thanked Speirs and drove home. She took a shower, washed her hair, and changed into one of her better pants suits. It was a size 16. Claire observed with sorrow that it was getting tight. In 1981, after Mrs. Quinton's health started to deteriorate, Claire had started to overeat. Most days, she drove to a

Burger King a few blocks from the apartment and ordered two chocolate shakes. During her visits to her mother at the hospital in January, Claire often went down to the coffee shop or to the vending machines for Coca-Colas and Milky Ways. In early 1981, she had weighed 135 pounds and had worn a size 12. On January 20, 1982, she weighed 185 pounds.

When Dwight Gaylord honked his car horn around six-forty-five that evening, Claire walked downstairs. Dwight drove his wife and sister-in-law to a steak house in Windsor Terrace. Dwight and Barbara ordered cocktails; Claire ordered a beer.

As Claire later recalled the conversation, Barbara said to her, "I will back you in any decision you make, but Mama belongs in a nursing home." When they were eating their steaks, Barbara looked at her sister and said, "Get yourself together, Claire. There are three things you have to do. Lose weight. Get a job. And get someone in to share the expenses of the apartment."

"What about Mama?" Claire asked Barbara.

"She'll be in a nursing home," Barbara answered.

"Only temporarily," Claire said.

"Forever," Barbara said.

"No way, nohow," Claire said. "Mama was too good to me when I was having my operations. No way could I just ship her off forever."

"I think you're making a big mistake, Claire," Barbara said.

Claire decided that it was pointless to pursue the subject with her sister. She had always found Barbara bossy and overbearing. For the rest of the meal, she talked to

Barbara and Dwight about their grown children, Charles, Sarah, and Elizabeth, of whom she is extremely fond. Afterward, the Gaylords drove Claire home. She walked upstairs slowly, dragging her right leg, which ached at the end of a long day. Before Claire went to bed, she prayed to God for guidance. She had once spent a year and a half in a convent. Claire goes to Mass six days a week and signs her letters "Love and Prayers." She is a great believer in prayer. "That night, I prayed and I prayed and I prayed," she later remembered.

CHAPTER TWO

ON JANUARY 21, Claire Quinton kept her appointment with Haydee Santana. She brought in all but one of the documents that Miss Santana had said were needed to establish proof of Mrs. Quinton's Medicaid eligibility; she brought in the missing document the following day, weeks before most of the people Miss Santana customarily dealt with, who were less well organized, would have done so. Three days later, Haydee Santana sent Mrs. Quinton's completed Medicaid application to the appropriate division of New York City's Human Resources Administration: the Medical Assistance Program.

January 21 was also the day Dr. Ruffolo received the results of Mrs. Quinton's gallbladder X-rays. He called in a surgeon, Dr. Amarendra Shah, for a consultation. Dr. Shah, who had removed the lump from Mrs. Quinton's breast the previous year, telephoned Claire that evening and told her that the gallbladder X-rays suggested that

Mrs. Quinton had gallstones. In his opinion, she required a gallbladder operation. Claire was upset about her mother's poor physical condition. If an operation would restore her to good health, she believed that it made sense. She said, however, that she doubted if her mother was strong enough for such an operation and that she doubted if her mother would consent to it. On January 22, Dr. Shah wrote on Mrs. Quinton's chart that she should have the upper-gastrointestinal series and the barium-enema series, which had not yet been done. That day, Mrs. Quinton's chart said "Very weak." She received a blood transfusion on January 22 and again on the twenty-seventh. She had the barium enema on January 30. Her colon was "unremarkable" except for the presence of di-verticula — numerous small pockets that had formed in the walls of the large intestine. Diverticula are present in about twenty to thirty percent of Americans over the age of fifty. The results of the upper-gastrointestinal series, done on February 1, were "WNL" — within normal limits. There was no evidence of anything untoward in Mrs. Quinton's esophagus, her stomach, or her duodenum: no ulcers, no tumors. On February 1, Dr. Ruffolo took a week's vacation; he left Mrs. Quinton in the hands of Dr. Shah and another colleague. When Dr. Ruffolo returned, on February 8, he reviewed Mrs. Quinton's chart. Al-though the urinary-tract infection with which she had been admitted had been resolved, she had developed another urinary-tract infection while he was away, but it was clearing up because of the tetracycline she was being given. The assorted X-ray series and blood tests to which she had been submitted between January 5 and February

1 had ruled out a renal malignancy and several other types of cancer, as well as hepatitis. Many of the X-rays showed that Mrs. Quinton had severe osteoarthritis — a chronic condition. On February 8, Dr. Ruffolo asked Mrs. Quinton if she wanted to undergo gallbladder surgery. She said emphatically that she did not. He pronounced Mrs. Quinton "medically cleared." This meant that there was nothing further he or the hospital could do to make a significant change in her condition.

Most patients who are medically cleared are discharged to their homes, as Mrs. Quinton had been in 1981 after the lump in her breast was removed. A small percentage of the patients admitted to Lutheran cannot be discharged home when they are medically cleared — mostly elderly patients whose condition has taken a turn for the worse in the hospital, as Mrs. Quinton's now had. Lutheran Medical Center is an acute-care hospital and is committed to using its beds for patients who require the treatment an acute-care hospital can give. A patient who has been medically cleared is considered to be at Lutheran inappropriately. He or she may be "blocking" a bed that could otherwise be used by a patient with acute needs; Lutheran's occupancy rate in 1982 was eighty-six percent. Medically cleared patients who remain at Lutheran are put on an "Alternate Level of Care" list; that means that they are awaiting transfer to alternative care at home or in another institution — a physical-rehabilitation facility, a terminal-care facility, or, most often, a nursing home. A few prosperous people on the alternative-care list go home and are cared for by nurses or home attendants for whom they pay privately. A number of patients who already have Medicaid are able to return home with the aid of home attendants paid for by the Human Resources Administration. Like the majority of people on the alternative-care list, Mrs. Quinton was covered by Medicare, which pays for a limited amount of home health care — a much more limited amount than Mrs. Quinton needed on February 8, 1982.

There are thirty patients on the alternative-care list at Lutheran on an average day; twenty-eight of them are waiting to get into nursing homes. Most of these patients stay in the limbo of alternative-care status for weeks or months, either because their applications for Medicaid are pending or because a place in a nursing home has not yet been found for them. The occupancy rate of nursing homes in New York City is close to one hundred percent, which enables nursing homes to be quite selective. Lutheran's situation is not unique. A 1980 one-day census of hospitals in New York State found approximately 4400 patients in alternative-care status. They used roughly seven percent of all acute-care beds and ran up unnecessary hospital charges of approximately $242 million a year.

On January 20, Bob Speirs had already started Mrs. Quinton on her way to a nursing home by helping Claire with her mother's Medicaid application. On January 22, he asked a discharge-planning nurse to fill out a form called a DMS-1 on Kate Quinton, to determine the level of care she needed. ("DMS" stands for Division of Medical Standards.) A DMS-1 is a tool used in New York State to judge a patient's ability to function physically and mentally; it tries to assess the level of nursing and custodial care he or she will require. Points are assigned for certain types of required treatment (75 points for round-the-clock inhalation treatment, 100 points for round-the-clock feeding) and for various types of behavior (50 points for being abusive at all times, 80 points for being assaultive at all times). Patients whose DMS-1 scores are between zero and 59 qualify for Domiciliary Care Facilities (adult homes). Those who score between 60 and 179 qualify for Health Related Facilities (intermediate-care homes). Those who score above 180 qualify for Skilled Nursing Facilities (nursing homes). The highest possible DMS-1 score is close to 1300 points. Mrs. Quinton's initial DMS-1 score was 283. On February 9, and every ten days thereafter, Bob Speirs had a discharge-planning nurse do another DMS-1 on Mrs. Quinton. Her score was 366 on February 9 and February 19, and 423 on March 1. She always received 105 points for being unable to walk. Her score was forty points lower whenever she required only "some help" rather than "total help" with dressing. A hundred points were added on March 1, when she developed bedsores that required frequent treatment. Mr. Speirs sent each of Mrs. Quinton's DMS-1 scores to twenty nursing homes. He telephoned ten nursing homes a week to see if one had a bed available for her. Medicare will reimburse a hospital for Alternate Level of Care days only in the case of patients who require skilled nursing care and only if a member of the Social Service Department documents on patients' charts his or her "diligent efforts" to secure nursing-home placement.

What Mrs. Quinton's DMS-1 forms didn't show but her chart did was her frame of mind. In early February, there were just two days when Mrs. Quinton's nurses reported her to be in good spirits — February 10 (the day before her birthday) and February 11. On the morning of the eleventh, Mrs. Quinton's grandson and his wife, who live in Arkansas, sent her a dozen long-stemmed red roses as their gift and a floral arrangement from their two small children. In the early afternoon, while Claire was visiting, Sally Thurman, Mrs. Quinton's primary-care nurse, came into the room with two other nurses. Mrs. Thurman was carrying a piece of cake on which she had put a candle. The three nurses sang "Happy Birthday." Mrs. Quinton, who was touched by this gesture, blew out the candle and ate some of the cake. Sally Thurman and Kate Quinton were two strong-willed women, but they both believed that some compromise was possible in life: Now when Mrs. Quinton was taken out of bed to sit in a chair, it was only for an hour and a half twice a day rather than three hours once a day. Her head no longer drooped onto the tray rest, and she complained less. In the late afternoon, after Claire had gone home, Barbara and Dwight Gaylord came to visit Kate Quinton for the second time, bringing with them their older daughter, Sarah, and her fiancé, Brian; one of Mrs. Quinton's sisters; two pounds of butter cookies; a bottle of champagne; and a package of plastic glasses. Barbara gave one pound of cookies to the nurses. Mrs. Quinton doesn't drink champagne, but she loves butter cookies, and she ate quite a few of them while her relatives drank a toast to her on her eightieth birthday.

For two weeks before her birthday and for two weeks afterward, Mrs. Quinton was extremely depressed. "Nurse, why me?" she asked one day in late January. "Just leave me alone," she said the next day, refusing to drink her citrate of magnesia and throwing it on the floor. Although Mrs. Quinton was put on a regular diet on February 10, which was to be supplemented with strawberry milkshakes, she ate sparingly. She was never weighed at Lutheran, but she appeared to lose a pound or two a week. She required one more blood transfusion. On several days in February, she refused to have blood drawn. Another day, she pulled out her catheter. The nurses, residents, and third-year medical students noted that "she feels helpless, feels very disgusted," and commented that she needed to be built up psychologically.

The most frequent exchange Mrs. Quinton had with Claire on her daily visits went like this:

"Are you sure I'm only going to go to a nursing home temporarily?"

"Mama, would I sell you a bill of goods?"

"I guess not, but those nursing homes I saw on television were so awful."

"Four to six weeks — eight weeks maximum."

Mrs. Quinton often called Claire at home to say, "Bring my clothes. Call an ambulance" or "Get me out of here. If I don't get out of this dive, I'll lose my mind."

One morning after her mother had called, Claire telephoned Barbara. As Claire recalls the conversation, Barbara asked, "Why are you bothering me when I'm on my way to work?"

"I'm calling now because I didn't want to bother you at work," Claire said. "Mama's upset. I know you call her every day after five, but I wish you'd call her today around ten-thirty to cheer her up a bit before I get there around two."

Barbara said goodbye without committing herself to telephoning at a particular time.

In mid-February, Claire Quinton got a recurrence of a bad case of flu she had had on and off from September to December of 1981. For about a week, she couldn't come to the hospital. Mrs. Quinton missed her company and the roast-beef sandwiches and rice pudding that Claire had begun bringing her from the delicatessen. On February 22, Mrs. Quinton was particularly downcast. Her feet were badly swollen. She attributed her lack of appetite to the "garbage food" served at Lutheran. That day, Bob Speirs wrote on Kate Quinton's chart, "Continuing to follow for NHP [nursing-home placement]. Medicaid still pending. No beds available as yet."

❧

On February 22, a seventy-one-year-old man named Gerald Cooper, who had been a patient at Lutheran since June and had been on the Alternate Level of Care list for four months, left the hospital. Mr. Cooper's right side had been severely weakened by a stroke he suffered in 1980. His left leg had been amputated above the knee in July. His latest DMS-1 score was 557. No nursing home had accepted him. He didn't want to go to a nursing home, and his wife, who was seventy-six and had visited him almost every day during his long hospitalization, didn't want him to go to one, either. She wanted to care for him at home. On February 22, Mr. and Mrs. Cooper got their wish. Gerald Cooper went home. He went home thanks to a program called Transitional Community Placement (T.C.P.), a collaboration between Lutheran Medical

Center and the New York City Department of City Planning.

The Transitional Community Placement program was the creation of Herbert Sturz, who had become chairman of the City Planning Commission in 1980. Mr. Sturz is a social reformer with somewhat catholic interests. He was director and president of the Vera Institute of Justice from its inception, in 1961, to 1977. (Vera is a nonprofit organization committed to improving the criminal-justice system). He is well known for his work in reforming the city's bail system, which led to the reform of the entire federal bail system, in the Federal Bail Reform Act of 1966. One of the many subjects he became interested in at Vera was home health care for the aged. He concluded that a lot of the aged were winding up in nursing homes prematurely and should be given a chance to be cared for in their own homes, because it was more humane. Sturz is a social reformer with a pragmatic approach. He knew that old people were more likely to be given this chance if it could be demonstrated that home care was less expensive than keeping them in Alternate Level of Care status until they were channeled into nursing homes.

The Department of City Planning had access to some Community Development money. Most C.D. money is spent on housing, streets, sewers, and the like, but there is a small amount that may be used for social services in designated areas, such as Sunset Park. Sturz perceived home health care as a social service. Howard Hornstein, one of the seven City Planning commissioners, is the treasurer of Lutheran Medical Center. Almost half the people who live in Sunset Park go to Lutheran when they require hospitalization. Hornstein arranged for Sturz to meet George Adams, the president of Lutheran. In 1980, 302 patients accounted for approximately 11,000 days of alternative care at Lutheran, at a total cost of about three million dollars. Mr. Adams was willing to work with City Planning on a program that would benefit the hospital and divert people from nursing homes.

In May of 1981, Sturz hired David Gould, a Vera project director who had acquired a fair amount of experience in the fields of home health care and employment of the hard-to-employ, to direct City Planning's Community Health and Employment Program. In June of 1981, Mr. Gould hired Diane Confalone as his assistant. Miss Confalone has a master's degree in public health and had just completed a year at Lutheran Medical Center as an administrative resident. Between June of 1981 and February of 1982, David Gould and Diane Confalone studied the way elderly patients left the hospital, and devised Transitional Community Placement as a way to help some patients on the alternative-care list waiting for nursing homes try home care instead. They decided to work with residents of Sunset Park and Bay Ridge. They chose people with low and moderate incomes, especially those with pending Medicaid applications; people who needed from twenty to eighty-four hours of home-care service a week from the program (they calculated that their budget would not be large enough to include patients who needed twenty-four-hour-a-day care); and people who couldn't be readily discharged to other existing programs, such as the Human Resources Administration's Home Attendant

Program, which was for those who already had Medicaid coverage.

During those eight months, Mr. Gould and Miss Confalone obtained grants from the United Hospital Fund of New York and the New York Community Trust to complement the Community Development money made available by the Department of City Planning. Sturz likes to take two social problems and fold them into a single solution. One of his favorite Vera programs is called Easyride. The Easyriders are homebound old people who are driven in vans to visit their doctors or to go shopping or to senior citizens' centers; the van drivers are ex-offenders or ex-addicts. Sunset Park is a predominantly Hispanic area, whose population has a high rate of unemployment. In January of 1982, Diane Confalone interviewed a number of unemployed women in Sunset Park who were interested in jobs as home attendants in preference to going on welfare. She recruited eight women to work as home attendants for Transitional Community Placement patients. Miss Confalone and Mr. Gould drew up a contract between Lutheran Medical Center and Family Home Care Services of Brooklyn and Queens — one of New York City's nonprofit "vendor" agencies that hire home attendants to serve Human Resources Administration (H.R.A.) clients — to employ, in addition, a small number of home attendants selected by T.C.P. for its patients. These vendor agencies are responsible for paying home attendants' wages and fringe benefits, withholding all required taxes, and recruiting, supervising, and replacing home attendants. One of the first eight women Diane Confalone selected was Belinda Fernández, a woman in her early forties who was born in Puerto Rico but spoke excellent English. Mrs. Fernández had recently been laid off from a job as a sewing-machine operator and was about to apply for unemployment insurance. On February 22, Belinda Fernández became Gerald Cooper's home attendant.

On February 19, when Diane Confalone asked Bob Speirs about possible T.C.P. patients, he recommended Kate Quinton. He told Miss Confalone a little about Kate Quinton's medical history and gave her Claire Quinton's telephone number. Diane Confalone called Claire Quinton that day and briefly described T.C.P. to her. Claire was home with the flu. "It's been difficult for me to take care of my mother at home," she told Miss Confalone. "She tied me to the house. She falls a lot. We were told last year that she needed special shoes to help her walk, but they cost two or three hundred dollars and she says she can't afford them. My mother admits that it takes two nurses to lift her out of bed. I've had five spinal fusions. I could never lift her. Our apartment is cold. The landlord doesn't heat it adequately. My mother spent last winter under an electric blanket. I'll think about the program, but I think a nursing home would be best for now."

On February 24, Miss Confalone ran into Bob Speirs in a hospital corridor. They spoke about Mr. Cooper and how happy he was to be home. Mr. Speirs again mentioned Kate Quinton, whose room was nearby. At four-thirty that afternoon, Diane Confalone walked into Kate Quinton's

room. It was bleak and silent. Mrs. Quinton's roommate
— her third since January — was asleep. Mrs. Quinton's
eyes were open, and she was lying in bed quietly, partly
covered by a sheet, sucking on a throat lozenge. She was
wearing a blue hospital gown and had white socks on
her feet, which were elevated on a pillow.

"How are you feeling today?" Diane Confalone asked.

"Look at my feet," Mrs. Quinton answered. She sat up
in bed and slowly removed the white anklets. Her feet
were badly swollen.

"They do seem to be swollen," Miss Confalone said.

"That's an understatement," Mrs. Quinton said. "The
left foot isn't just swollen, it's deformed. It's been that
way since I was born. It was operated on in 1921. The
operation was a complete failure. Arthritis has made my
feet much worse."

"Are you getting physical therapy for your feet?" Miss
Confalone asked.

"No, and I think I need some," Mrs. Quinton answered.

Mrs. Quinton's arms and legs were spindly and her face
was wan. Although she looked to Miss Confalone like a
very sick woman, her watery greengage eyes seemed in-
telligent and her manner alert. Miss Confalone was convinced that Mrs. Quinton had had an operation on her
left foot in 1921 — not in 1920 or 1922.

"I miss my daughter's visits," Mrs. Quinton said, as if
eager to continue the conversation with this pretty young
stranger, whose name she didn't seem to have any need
to know. Mrs. Quinton liked to talk; she didn't like to
lie in semidarkness looking at closets A and B or watching

the hands on the hall clock in slow motion. When their eyes met, Kate Quinton said directly to Diane Confalone, "I want to go home."

Mrs. Quinton struck Diane Confalone as a good candidate for Transitional Community Placement. She didn't mention the program to her, because she didn't want to give her any false hopes. She had already learned that patients' relatives had more to say than the patients themselves did about whether they went home or to nursing homes. She thanked Mrs. Quinton for talking to her, admired a plant on her windowsill, and went downstairs to call Claire Quinton. "I've seen your mother, and she wants to go home," Miss Confalone said. She asked Claire if she would be willing to come to her office at Lutheran the following day to hear more about the program. Claire was over the worst of the flu and had been planning to visit her mother on February 25. She said she would stop at Miss Confalone's office.

⋘

Claire Quinton limped into Diane Confalone's office on the twenty-fifth. Miss Confalone helped her remove her coat and offered her a chair. Claire sat down cautiously, putting her pocketbook and shopping bag on the floor and holding her metal cane. She looked weary but friendly. Miss Confalone told her she would explain the components of the program. First, she spoke about the daily home attendant that Mrs. Quinton would have. Then she explained that Cindy Strong, the program's public-health nurse, would come to the Quintons' home as often as Mrs. Quinton needed her. Miss Strong would supervise Mrs.

Quinton's medication and work with Claire and the home attendant to devise Mrs. Quinton's plan of care. Miss Confalone then asked Claire if her mother had a private doctor who made home visits. Claire said that Dr. Ruffolo had come to the house six times in 1981. Miss Confalone said that T.C.P. made physical-therapy referrals to Nursing Sisters Home Visiting Service, a certified home health agency. Claire Quinton said she would appreciate such a referral. Her mother had had a physical therapist from Nursing Sisters in 1981. Miss Confalone said that T.C.P. would provide transportation home from the hospital for Mrs. Quinton, and medical equipment and other supplies. Minor housing repairs could be made and heavy-duty cleaning could be done, if necessary. "Those are the components of the Transitional Community Placement program, and it lasts three months," she said. "During those three months, we'll be working continually with your mother to develop a long-term-care plan that will take over after the three months are up. I hope by then her Medicaid will be in place. While your mother is on T.C.P., Cindy will continue to fill out DMS-1 forms, and Lutheran's Social Service Department will send them to nursing homes, so if you should decide that home care isn't viable you'll still have that option if a nursing home accepts her. This is a pilot program, and we'll be keeping a close watch on your mother. If you both decide to try T.C.P. and we accept your mother, she'll be our second patient. Do you think this is something you'd like to consider?"

"Yes, I would," Claire Quinton said.

"Where do you live?" Diane Confalone asked.

"Two ninety-two Seeley Street, in Windsor Terrace," Claire answered.

Miss Confalone asked Claire to speak to Cindy Strong and went to get her.

Cindy Strong came into the office and asked Claire Quinton a few questions about her mother's ailments and Medicaid status. She also asked Claire how she had managed to take care of her mother before Mrs. Quinton entered the hospital in January. Claire told her that a home-care worker from a special program sponsored by Selfhelp Community Services had come twice a week for two hours since the spring of 1981. The home-care worker had bathed her mother, changed her bed, done the heavy cleaning, helped her exercise her legs, and chatted with her.

"What did you do all the other hours of the week?" Miss Strong asked.

"I struggled," Claire answered.

"I see you have a cane," Miss Strong said. "How's your health?"

"I've had five spinal fusions. I haven't been able to work for the past six years, partly because of my back and partly because . . ." Claire's voice faded.

"How many hours a day do you think your mother would require a home attendant?"

"Eight hours a day, seven days a week, from ten in the morning until six in the evening."

"Why would you want the home attendant to start at ten, and not at nine?"

"My mother has insomnia. Sometimes she doesn't fall into a deep sleep until five o'clock in the morning, but then she sleeps for a good five hours."

"Is there any equipment your mother needs and doesn't have?"

"A hospital bed and a wheelchair. We already have a walker and a commode."

"Would you send your mother to a nursing home?"

"I'd considered it, because I felt I couldn't handle her all by myself, but I've been uneasy about sending her to a nursing home, because she's dead set against it."

"It sounds as if your mother might be a good candidate for the Day Hospital program at Metropolitan Jewish Geriatric Center."

"We live on the second floor. My mother can't go downstairs."

"Do you have any relatives who can help you take care of your mother?"

"I have a sister in New Jersey, but we don't see too much of her. She went back to work part time when her youngest child was eight, because she was afraid that otherwise she'd become a canasta bum. She and her husband are pretty social. They go to lots of cocktail parties and they like the golf club. They're planning to move to Arizona in a few years."

"What about neighbors?"

"A few years ago, we had an apartment at 283 Seeley. We're on good terms with the people we shared the house with. They'd help me in an emergency. So would my landlord. When his wife came home from the hospital, I took her two meals a day and checked on her four times a day while he was at work. The only thing he won't do is give us enough heat. The thermostat is in his apartment."

"How much rent do you pay?"

"Three hundred and forty-five dollars a month, but my mother thinks we pay three hundred. He raised us forty-five dollars last September, and, what with the lack of heat, I haven't had the courage to tell her."

Cindy Strong told Claire she would do a nursing assessment on Mrs. Quinton the following morning, and excused herself. Diane Confalone returned. By then, she had studied a map of Brooklyn and had decided that 292 Seeley was close enough to Sunset Park for T.C.P. to include Mrs. Quinton. Miss Confalone asked if it would be convenient for Claire if she and David Gould and Cindy Strong made a home visit on the twenty-sixth, in the early afternoon. Claire was amenable.

ᐖᎮ

On February 26, Claire Quinton showed Diane Confalone, David Gould, and Cindy Strong around the apartment. Mrs. Quinton had a large bedroom with two twin beds. Claire's small bedroom contained one. The kitchen was spacious, the bathroom modern, the living room comfortable. The style of the cherry-finished mahogany furniture suggested it was fifty years old, but years of careful polishing made the highboy, the desk, the chest of drawers, the dresser, the night table, the tip table, and the drum table look better than new. The purpose of the visit was to determine whether the patient would be returning to a suitable environment. Mrs. Quinton obviously would be. Later that afternoon, Diane Confalone and Cindy Strong met with Dr. Ruffolo at his office, in Bensonhurst. They wanted his support for Mrs. Quinton's discharge to

Transitional Community Placement. He said he would give it, but not before telling them that he believed that both Claire and Kate had a drinking problem, and that he no longer had time to make house calls in Windsor Terrace, because it was too far from his office and his practice had become too busy.

On February 25, after her meetings with Diane Confalone and Cindy Strong, Claire Quinton was convinced that T.C.P. would accept her mother. She went directly to Room 5911, took a pastrami sandwich and a bottle of ginger ale out of her shopping bag, and put them down on her mother's night table. She kissed her mother on the cheek, sat down, took her hand, and described T.C.P. to Mrs. Quinton just as Miss Confalone had described it to her. "I think it's the answer to my prayers," she said.

Mrs. Quinton's eyes glistened, and, for once, the tears seemed unrelated to her need for new eyeglasses. "Oh, Claire, do you really mean it?" she said. "I've been praying since January that I wouldn't have to go to a nursing home."

Claire telephoned Barbara to tell her about her decision to take her mother home on T.C.P., described the program to her, and again said she believed that it was the unexpected answer to her prayers. Claire had hoped that Barbara would say something like "That's terrific." Instead, she later recalled, Barbara was uncharacteristically silent. To Claire, Barbara's silence implied disapproval.

At nine o'clock the following evening, the telephone rang. It was Dwight Gaylord. Claire's recollection of the conversation is that Dwight Gaylord told her, "Your mother's sick. She belongs in a nursing home with people her own age. She's senile, and besides that she's nothing but a bitch." Claire hung up. "I suppose I hung up instead of telling him off because I couldn't quite believe what I was hearing," she said later.

When Claire visited her mother at the hospital the following afternoon, she couldn't keep from telling her about Dwight's phone call.

"These things really hurt when you can't retaliate," Mrs. Quinton said. "When I feel well, I'll get back at that rat."

Barbara Gaylord expressed her opposition to T.C.P. by calling Bob Speirs. According to Speirs, she told him she thought that her mother belonged in a nursing home.

It was the first time Bob Speirs had had any contact with Barbara. "I've been dealing with your sister," he told her.

"Oh, you really can't trust her," Barbara said. "She's a drunk. She's crazy. She can't take care of Mother." Mr. Speirs was glad that Barbara's comments stopped there. He had no desire to become involved in a family dispute. He noticed that Barbara had spoken only of what Claire couldn't do, and not of what Barbara would be willing to do for her mother.

Bob Speirs had taken a liking to Kate Quinton. He had read on her record that she was born in Scotland, and had told her that his father was born in the Scottish village of Dalmuir, which proved to be only a few miles from Mrs. Quinton's birthplace. Mr. Speirs noticed that she always had a pleasant word for him. Claire Quinton had also impressed him favorably. He sensed that she cared about her mother, despite her own problems. She didn't complain about her back. She didn't have to. The pain on her face spoke for itself. Claire had looked into the four nursing homes in Brooklyn that were checked off on the list Bob Speirs had given her on January 20, and had told him she would want her mother to go to only one of them — Cobble Hill, a nursing home near Brooklyn Heights, one of the nicest sections of the borough. She said that the mother of an acquaintance of hers was in Cobble Hill and that the acquaintance thought highly of it. She didn't share with Bob Speirs her reasons for not wanting her mother to go to any of the three other nursing homes. One was in a bad neighborhood; she felt that it would be unsafe to park her car there. Two were in predominantly Jewish neighborhoods; she assumed that their clientele would also be predominantly Jewish and that her mother wouldn't fit in, and she also assumed that both homes served kosher food. In January 1977, Claire had broken her right ankle and right leg and had been taken to Maimonides Hospital, which served only kosher food. She had kept the milk that came with dairy meals, and her three roommates' containers of milk, on the windowsill near the bed, so that she could drink milk when a meat meal was served. She knew that when her mother ate meat and vegetables she also liked to have a potato with butter and bread with butter.

It was clear to Bob Speirs that Kate Quinton was a good candidate for a nursing home. Patients with DMS-1 scores of over 500 points were usually harder to place — especially those who needed highly sophisticated life-support systems — and so were patients whose behavior was abusive or assaultive. Mr. Speirs had never been to Cobble Hill. He and his four coworkers in Lutheran's Social Service Department had little time to go into the field. In four years at Lutheran, he had become accustomed to sending patients to nursing homes he had never seen. The director of Social Service had visited many nursing homes over the years, and Speirs and the other members of the staff relied on his appraisals and on word of mouth from the families of patients they had previously placed. Lutheran sent its "best" patients to one nursing home on Staten Island and to several nursing homes in Brooklyn. This was done because Lutheran's Social Service Department had good rapport with the directors of admission of these particular homes, and the homes knew that Lutheran's DMS-1 forms were done honestly. Nursing-home personnel rarely came to Lutheran to look at patients, but they often spoke to the relatives of patients whose admissions they were considering. Bob Speirs knew that Claire would make a favorable impression at Cobble Hill. Legally, an alternative-care patient at Lutheran must go to the first nursing home within a fifty-mile radius that offers a place, and occasionally patients are sent to homes they don't want to go to. Bob Speirs thought Mrs. Quinton had a good chance of being accepted at Cobble Hill. When he had discussed her case with Cobble Hill's director of admissions in February, she had told him she thought she would have a bed for Mrs. Quinton relatively soon. Cobble Hill was one of three or four nursing homes on Lutheran's list that accepted Medicaid-pending patients. Still, Bob Speirs knew that Mrs. Quinton couldn't reconcile herself to going to a nursing home, and so he had suggested to Diane Confalone that she evaluate her for T.C.P.

By Monday, March 1, almost everything was set for Mrs. Quinton to go home on T.C.P. on March 3. Her catheter, which she had had since January 6, was removed. The hospital bed and the wheelchair had been ordered for delivery to her home on March 2. Cindy Strong had decided that Mrs. Quinton needed a home attendant fifty-six hours a week. Diane Confalone had asked Evelyn Partisi, a case coordinator at Family Home Care, to get in touch with Lolita López, one of the eight home attendants she had chosen. On March 2, Bob Speirs received a call from the director of admissions at Cobble Hill. There was a bed available for Kate Quinton. He went upstairs to 5911 to tell Kate and Claire Quinton that they now had a choice: Mrs. Quinton could go to Cobble Hill on March 3 or she could go home. They chose home. Speirs informed Dr. Ruffolo of their decision; he sensed that Dr. Ruffolo would have preferred to have Mrs. Quinton go to Cobble Hill. Dr. Ruffolo later told Diane Confalone he believed that Kate Quinton belonged in a nursing home permanently because Claire's own limitations made her unable to take care of her headstrong mother. Bob Speirs called Cobble Hill's director to tell her of the Quintons' decision; she said that Mrs. Quinton could apply to Cobble Hill again if she changed her mind. Bob Speirs was pleased that Kate Quinton was going home. He thought she would be better off there. He didn't like to see a keen eighty-year-old woman sent to a nursing home against her will. He knew that some patients — particularly those who went to nursing homes for a rehabilitative stay after a broken hip — later returned home, but he also knew that seventy-five percent did not.

Claire Quinton appeared in Diane Confalone's office on the morning of March 3. She looked fearful. "I just don't think I can manage my mother by myself," she said. Miss Confalone and Cindy Strong talked to her for a while. They assured her that she wouldn't be by herself — that she would have a lot of help and support. They asked if she would prefer to wait a day or two. "No, I guess I just have cold feet," Claire said. "I guess I'll be able to manage." She went to the cashier's window to pay her mother's telephone bill, which came to $82.50. Then she went up to her mother's room, then back down to Diane Confalone's office. She was carrying the plant that had been on her mother's windowsill. "Thank you for all you've done for us," she said, as she handed Miss Confalone the plant. The ambulance that Diane Confalone had ordered arrived on time. Mrs. Quinton and Claire were home at eleven-thirty. The ambulance attendants attempted to put Mrs. Quinton in the hospital bed, which stood in her bedroom in the place formerly occupied by one of the twin beds. (The twin bed was now stored behind her dresser.) She refused to get into bed and insisted on being put in her wheelchair.

Claire Quinton had expected a home attendant to be on her doorstep. None was there. She telephoned Diane Confalone in the early afternoon. "So where's my help?" she inquired. Miss Confalone told Claire she didn't know but would find out. She telephoned a while later to say that a home attendant would be there at ten o'clock the next morning. Cindy Strong visited the Quintons at four o'clock. She found Mrs. Quinton in her wheelchair, puffing on a cigarette. Mrs. Quinton hadn't been permitted to smoke in her hospital bed. Miss Strong chided her for smoking the day she got home. "I don't inhale," Mrs. Quinton said. "Besides, when you can do as little as I can, you've got to do something wicked." Miss Strong told Mrs. Quinton that she had been up long enough, and that she would help her into bed. Mrs. Quinton reluctantly agreed to let Miss Strong transfer her from her wheelchair to her bed. She gave Miss Strong little assistance. Cindy Strong helped her onto the bedpan, which was kept on the commode next to the hospital bed. She was concerned about Mrs. Quinton's swollen legs and feet and about bedsores on her buttocks. She advised Mrs. Quinton to turn from side to side every two hours and to stay off her back. She asked Claire to buy some Vaseline and apply it to her mother's chafed skin. She said she would visit again the next morning. That evening, Claire gave her mother a light dinner in bed. Before Mrs. Quinton went to sleep, she said, "Thanks be to God. It's so good to be back in our own home again."

CHAPTER THREE

THE HOME ATTENDANT WHO CAME to the Quintons' at ten o'clock on March 4 was not one of the eight women Diane Confalone had screened. Evelyn Partisi had been unable to reach Lolita López; she had got a job as a nurse's aide between the time Miss Confalone interviewed her and the time Miss Partisi tried to call her. In 1982, Family Home Care had about 1150 clients from the Human Resources Administration's home-care program — 950 in Brooklyn and 200 in Queens. Each of its ten coordinators handled about 115 cases. By the end of March, Evelyn Partisi had four T.C.P. cases in addition to her 115 cases. The rate of turnover was rapid. Some clients became too ill to stay at home and went into hospitals or nursing homes, or they died; new clients replaced them. At any one time, Family Home Care used about 1500 home attendants. These home attendants came and went, often going to jobs that paid better than the minimum wage that Family Home Care paid. The names on the case coordinators' Cardexes were rarely the same two days in a row. Evelyn Partisi was constantly on the telephone, assigning and reassigning home attendants. She assigned Mercedes Robbins, the first home attendant she could reach, to Kate Quinton and asked her to go to 292 Seeley on March 3. When Miss Robbins failed to show up that day, Miss Partisi asked her to report to work on March 4.

Mercedes Robbins, a tall, willowy woman in her early twenties, arrived at the Quintons' at ten o'clock on March 4 wearing designer jeans and high-heeled boots. She was carrying a number of textbooks. By the time Cindy Strong got there, forty minutes later, Miss Robbins had helped Mrs. Quinton out of her flannel nightgown, given her a sponge bath, helped her put on underclothes, a shift, and a sweater, assisted her onto the commode, transferred her into her wheelchair, and emptied the bedpan and the commode. Miss Strong reviewed Miss Robbins's duties with her in Kate and Claire Quinton's presence. She had sixteen "personal care" duties, which included giving Mrs. Quinton a daily bath and a weekly shampoo. She also had twelve "household functions," which included vacuuming and sweeping, wet and dry mopping (in every room except Claire's), and ironing and mending for Mrs. Quinton. Cindy Strong instructed Mrs. Quinton to keep her legs elevated, and not to use salt in her diet, because of the edema. Mrs. Quinton was cheerful. "I could hardly wait to get out of bed this morning," she told Miss Strong. She refused to return to bed until the early afternoon. After Cindy Strong left, Miss Robbins rinsed Mrs. Quinton's nightgown, made her bed, and did some dusting. She then left Mrs. Quinton in her wheelchair in the dinette, where she preferred to sit, went into the Quintons' living room, turned on the color television set, and sat on the living-room sofa reading the books she had brought.

The following day, when Miss Strong visited, Mrs. Quinton was already in her wheelchair. She had to be persuaded to return to bed, so that Miss Strong could watch Mercedes transfer her from the wheelchair to the bed and could teach the Quintons and Miss Robbins some exercises that Mrs. Quinton was supposed to do to keep her legs from atrophying any further. After two months of lying in bed in the hospital, Kate Quinton's legs were, as she put it, "as limp as wet noodles."

On Monday, March 8, when Miss Strong arrived Mrs. Quinton was in bed. She said she didn't feel well and was too weak to get out of bed. Miss Strong telephoned Dr. Ruffolo. He told her to call a lab that would send someone to the Quintons' apartment the next day to do a complete blood count, a urinalysis, and some other tests on Mrs. Quinton. Mrs. Quinton also stayed in bed on the ninth. On the tenth, Dr. Ruffolo informed Miss Strong that Mrs. Quinton had a urinary-tract infection, and prescribed a medication to clear it up. On the eleventh, when Miss Strong arrived shortly after ten, Mrs. Quinton said that she felt better, but that her appetite was poor and she found the hospital bed uncomfortable. Its mattress was too hard. Mrs. Quinton was waiting for Mercedes Robbins to come; Miss Robbins had started showing up at ten-twenty or ten-thirty instead of at ten o'clock after her second day of work. The following week, the Quintons told Miss Strong that they were dissatisfied with Mercedes Robbins. When Claire had asked her to clean the Quintons' self-defrosting refrigerator — one of her twelve "household functions" — she had asked Claire to turn off the refrigerator, so that she wouldn't catch a cold. She had cleaned the refrigerator as she did most of her other tasks — capably and grudgingly. A nurse from Nursing Sisters Home Visiting Service who came on March 11 to evaluate Mrs. Quinton for physical therapy noted, "Home attendant appeared uninterested."

Claire knew that another of Miss Robbins's duties was to provide companionship to her mother, an outgoing woman. Claire occasionally went into the living room, asked Mercedes whether she minded if she turned off the TV for a while, and attempted to strike up a conversation with her, in the hope of encouraging Mercedes to talk to her mother. Claire learned that Mercedes Robbins had been born in Guinea or Guyana — she almost always mumbled, and Claire wasn't sure of the country — and that she had a five-year-old son, whom her mother cared for. Mercedes went to high school at night and was studying bookkeeping, typing, and English. She was disinclined to talk. She tended to express herself in monosyllables. Her favorites were "Uh" and "Huh." She never referred to her son by name and showed little interest in anything but watching television and leaving early. During Mrs. Quinton's first two weeks at home, she went to bed at five o'clock. Claire served her a light dinner, usually soup, in bed. Mercedes had her coat on at five-forty.

On March 18, Cindy Strong told Diane Confalone that the Quintons needed another home attendant, preferably someone who was older and more talkative. Miss Confalone called Evelyn Partisi and asked her to assign Alice Kuster, another of the first eight women she had recruited, to Kate Quinton, starting Monday, March 22. When Mercedes Robbins left the Quintons' apartment on the nineteenth, she said to them, in perfectly clear English, "When one door closes, another door opens."

Alice Kuster did not appear at the Quintons' on the morning of the twenty-second. Miss Confalone discovered that she hadn't been given proper directions and hadn't been able to find 292 Seeley Street. Miss Kuster wasn't very talkative anyway, so Miss Confalone asked Evelyn Partisi to assign Tina Ortiz, another of her first interviewees, to Mrs. Quinton, starting on March 23. Mrs. Ortiz was a pleasant, efficient, talkative woman in her early forties, whom Kate and Claire Quinton liked at once. When Claire learned where she lived and that she had come to the Quintons' by bus, she told Tina Ortiz that the trip was much shorter by subway. The token booth at the subway station nearest the Quintons' closed at 1:15 P.M. Mrs. Ortiz didn't have a token. Claire lent her one. Tina Ortiz called on the twenty-fourth to say she couldn't work that day, because her son had been in a car accident and had been rushed to the hospital. Mrs. Ortiz had liked the Quintons. She wrote Claire a nice note, in which she enclosed a token to replace the one she had borrowed. A week later, Tina Ortiz took a job in a hospital as a nurse's aide. On the twenty-fourth, Diane Confalone proposed Gabrielle Dumas, yet another of the first eight women she had recruited, to Evelyn Partisi for Mrs. Quinton, but Miss Dumas was unavailable. Miss Partisi assigned Felicity Sánchez, a young woman from El Salvador, to Mrs. Quinton.

The weekend home attendants who worked for the Quintons in March were as transitory as the weekday home attendants. Mercedes Robbins had come on Saturday and Sunday, March 6 and 7, because Evelyn Partisi had no time to recruit anyone else. Xaviera Johnson, a Jamaican in her late teens, had come on March 13 and 14. Miss Johnson amused Mrs. Quinton by asking her how she wheeled herself down the stairs, but she did not seem up to the job. Margaret Clayton, an American-born woman in her mid-thirties, who came to the Quintons' on Saturday, March 20, looked promising. She arrived in a pretty dress and high heels and immediately changed into a white dress and flat shoes. She went about her work proficiently and made pleasant conversation. She told Mrs. Quinton that she sewed all her own clothes and that she had graduated from a Seventh-Day Adventist college. Margaret Clayton asked Claire if she read the Bible, and questioned her about her religious faith. On Sunday the twenty-first, Claire Quinton went to the twelve-thirty Mass at Immaculate Heart of Mary with her best friend, Helen Durbin. When she got home, her mother was in bed. Claire was surprised — Mrs. Quinton hadn't taken any naps since leaving the hospital. Margaret Clayton was sitting in the living room reading her Bible and listening to gospel music on the radio. Claire went into her mother's bedroom and found out that after her departure Margaret Clayton had asked Mrs. Quinton to show her how to turn on the radio in the living room. The loud religious music had got on Mrs. Quinton's nerves, and she had taken refuge in bed. Claire asked Mrs. Clayton to please turn off the music and help her mother out of bed. The three women sat together in the kitchen. Margaret Clayton expressed concern about Claire's back and again spoke to Claire about the Bible, the church, God, and love. She left a few pamphlets about Seventh-Day Adventism for Claire to read.

The following Saturday, Claire gave Margaret Clayton a few booklets about Catholic missions. Around lunchtime, Mrs. Clayton said to Claire, "This afternoon, while your mother is resting, you and I are going to sit down on the living-room sofa, hold hands, and pray that you will be healed." Claire told Margaret Clayton that that would be very nice, except that she had other plans. She was going to attend four-o'clock Mass. Windsor Terrace is a predominantly Italian neighborhood. The four-o'clock Mass at Immaculate Heart of Mary is in Italian. To Claire, listening to Mass in a language she did not understand was preferable to a faith-healing session in her living room. On Sunday the twenty-eighth, Claire went to the twelve-thirty Mass with Helen Durbin. When she returned, Margaret Clayton was again playing gospel music, which was again driving Mrs. Quinton crazy. "You know how much I believe in my faith," Mrs. Clayton said to Claire that afternoon. "Seventh-Day Adventists observe the Sabbath on Saturday. I like to go to church on Saturday for three hours. Do you mind if I send my Aunt Nellie in my place next Saturday? It's all right with Evelyn Partisi. When I get my paycheck, I share it with Aunt Nellie." Two days later, Claire spoke to Cindy Strong. She told her about Margaret Clayton's Aunt Nellie and about the religious music that disturbed her mother. Miss Strong said she knew of an excellent home attendant who was available on weekends — Belinda Fernández, who worked for Gerald Cooper from Monday to Friday. Mrs. Cooper didn't want a home attendant to come in on weekends. She had an independent nature and believed she could take care of her husband on Saturday and Sunday with the help of her son and her grandson. Belinda Fernández wanted to earn additional money. Claire said she would be glad to have her. Miss Strong called Evelyn Partisi, who made arrangements for Belinda Fernández to start working for Kate Quinton the following Saturday.

Claire Quinton was pleased to see Felicity Sánchez, the new weekday home attendant, on March 25. Her back was sore from lifting her mother on the twenty-second and the twenty-fourth, when she had been without a home attendant. Felicity Sánchez was twenty-four and inexperienced, but her attitude was an improvement over Mercedes Robbins's. When Claire asked Felicity to clean the refrigerator, she took a damp sponge and started to wipe the refrigerator walls. Claire gave her a lesson in refrigerator cleaning. The first step, she explained, was to take all the food out of the refrigerator. The second was to remove the refrigerator grates and the vegetable bins and to wash them in warm soapy water; a Brillo pad might be needed on the grates. Step three was to dry the grates and bins. And so on. Felicity always had to be reminded to clean the refrigerator, but from then on she cleaned it Claire's way. Felicity seemed content to talk to Mrs. Quinton about her husband, who earned three hundred dollars a week working in New Jersey and got home at

8 P.M.; about her two small daughters, Elena and Rosalie; and about the city-subsidized babysitter who cared for the girls every day for the low sum of eight dollars a week. Felicity did the heavy cleaning lightly. She mopped the linoleum kitchen floor in haste with Spic and Span two or three times a week. Mrs. Quinton apologized to her visitors for its failure to shine the way kitchen floors had always shone wherever she kept house for over fifty years; she had got down on her hands and knees to buff them herself. But Felicity was willing, and that made Mrs. Quinton willing to overlook her shortcomings.

Belinda Fernández's work met Mrs. Quinton's high standards. The first Saturday she came, she noticed that Mrs. Quinton was looking at something in the kitchen.

"What are you staring at, Kate?" she asked.

"The valance over the kitchen sink," Mrs. Quinton answered. "It's greasy."

"I'll take care of it at once," Belinda said. "What else?"

"Well, the bedroom curtains could be dipped in water." They were.

Mrs. Fernández insisted on changing Kate Quinton's bed linen every Saturday and Sunday. She washed the sheets and pillowcases in the kitchen sink and hung them out on the line to dry. She washed Mrs. Quinton's hair and put it up in pin curls every Saturday and combed it out on Sunday. She massaged Mrs. Quinton's legs. She watched Mass on television with her every Sunday morning.

Thanks in large part to Felicity Sánchez and Belinda Fernández, April was a better month for Mrs. Quinton. In late March, she had had a toe infection. Cindy Strong had found a podiatrist, Dr. Andrew Beyer, who was willing to make house calls. Dr. Ruffolo had declined to prescribe diuretics for Mrs. Quinton when Cindy Strong called Mrs. Quinton's edema to his attention in early March. When she conveyed Dr. Beyer's concern about Mrs. Quinton's edema to his attention, he did prescribe diuretics, and her feet and legs gradually became less swollen. Evan Flint, the physical therapist from Nursing Sisters who had helped Mrs. Quinton get back on her feet when she was ill in 1981, began working with her again in late March. By mid-April, Kate Quinton was able to walk about fifteen feet, using her walker, with some assistance from Evan Flint.

During her first six weeks on T.C.P., Mrs. Quinton was not a compliant patient. Miss Strong urged her to keep the rails of the hospital bed up at night, so that she wouldn't fall out of bed; she said the rails made her feel too confined, and kept them down. Cindy Strong told her to elevate her feet when she sat in her wheelchair; every time Miss Strong visited, Mrs. Quinton's feet were on the floor. Mrs. Quinton said her legs got too tired on the wheelchair leg rests. She complained to Cindy Strong that she was lonely and depressed. Barbara, who had telephoned her every day while she was in the hospital, telephoned less frequently, didn't visit, and wanted her in a nursing home. Miss Strong suggested that Mrs. Quinton go to the Metropolitan Jewish Geriatric Center's Day Hospital for "socialization." Sitting around talking to other elderly people about their aches and pains was not the sort of socializing Mrs. Quinton cared to do. When Mrs. Quinton complained about her inability to read, because of her need for new eyeglasses, Miss Strong offered her Talking Books; she declined them. When Cindy Strong reminded Mrs. Quinton of the importance of keeping on a high-calorie, high-protein, low-fat diet, Mrs. Quinton said she had no appetite.

In late April, Kate Quinton became more cooperative. She didn't use the wheelchair leg rests, but she started to put her feet up on an ottoman she kept under the dinette table. She had solved the mattress problem by having a neighbor remove the hard hospital mattress and replace it with her own soft mattress. After a month of wearing socks but no shoes, she decided to wear shoes, to help herself walk. She had had enough of wearing shifts and started to wear dresses. She pronounced her hair a sorry sight and paid a friend of Felicity's, who was a beautician, to come to the house to give her a permanent. One day in late March, Mrs. Quinton had said to Claire, "No more of this eating in bed at five-thirty," and began to eat dinner with Claire in the kitchen at six-thirty, after watching the news on Claire's portable black-and-white TV set. By late April, Mrs. Quinton was able to assist in transferring herself from her wheelchair to her bed, and Claire was able to help her into bed at seven o'clock, when Mrs. Quinton's back hurt and she could no longer sit up.

By April, Kate Quinton had devised the following diet for herself:

10:30 A.M.: Breakfast — a cream-cheese-and-strawberry-preserves sandwich on white bread, two cups of Sanka with milk and sugar.

Noon to 12:45 P.M.: Lunch — an eggnog, composed of

twelve ounces of milk, one egg, and three ounces of Gallo cream sherry.

1:00 P.M. to 5:00 P.M.: A large bottle of ginger ale.

5:00 P.M. to 6:30 P.M.: Three ounces of sherry, to which Mrs. Quinton gradually added twenty-four ounces of ginger ale, orange soda, root beer, or any other soda that was in the house.

6:30 P.M.: Dinner — usually meat or fish, a vegetable, and a potato.

One morning, Cindy Strong asked Mrs. Quinton what she had eaten for dinner the previous evening. "Chicken, yams, and dull string beans," Mrs. Quinton said. "Claire's not nearly the cook I was. She forgot to put a pinch of baking soda into the boiling water before she put the string beans in. Baking soda makes them greener. You should always have a colorful plate. Pale-golden chicken, orange yams, and bright-green beans are an appealing sight."

Belinda Fernández telephoned Cindy Strong one Monday in April. She was upset by the amount of Gallo cream sherry that Mrs. Quinton was drinking. Miss Strong ran into Dr. Ruffolo, who told her that Mrs. Quinton could have an eggnog with sherry during the day and from one to two ounces of sherry in the evening. He said he doubted whether T.C.P. would be able to limit Mrs. Quinton's alcohol intake. Cindy Strong then spoke to Mrs. Quinton. "Sherry is only seventeen percent alcohol" and "I'll drink what I want" were Mrs. Quinton's final words on the matter. Belinda began to have a glass of sherry with Mrs. Quinton on weekends. On Mother's Day, she brought Mrs.

Quinton a present — a bottle of sherry. Claire Quinton had given up beer for Lent. Belinda Fernández and Felicity called Claire's beer drinking to Cindy Strong's attention after Easter. When Miss Strong relayed their concern to Dr. Ruffolo, he said, "Both Kate and Claire drink gin when they can get it." The two home attendants admitted that Claire never seemed adversely affected by the beer she drank and that she never neglected her mother. Miss Strong told them that Claire's beer drinking was her own business.

April was a better month for Claire Quinton, too. In March, she hadn't slept well, because she had always wondered whether her mother would call during the night to ask help to get onto the bedpan. She had hesitated to go out of the house while Mercedes Robbins was there, except to do the grocery shopping and to go to church, because she wasn't convinced that Mercedes would hear her mother if she called out while Mercedes was doing her homework and watching television. Claire's weight had continued to go up while her mother was in the hospital — at the end of February, she weighed 215 pounds — but then it started to go down, and in April she weighed 180. By April, Mrs. Quinton could get onto the bedpan alone. Claire still slept with her bedroom door open, but she slept more soundly. Felicity was dependable, so Claire felt more freedom to come and go. When her friend Veronica O'Connell, a schoolteacher on Long Island, came to stay with the Quintons for four days starting on the Thursday after Easter, Claire enjoyed going with her to see *On Golden Pond* and *Chariots of Fire* and driving her to Sunset Park to look at the house in which Veronica had been born. Claire's friend Helen Durbin had a washing machine. Claire took her laundry to Helen's house or to a Laundromat. Every week or two, she went to the bank. Once a month, she went to a local doctor for a Vitamin B_{12} shot, and in April, when she developed a dry cough, she went to see him about that. Once a month, Claire went to see a psychiatrist (for medication) and a psychotherapist (for therapy) at a mental-health clinic. She had become depressed in 1976 and had been taking medication and receiving therapy ever since.

✌⧹

One day in early April, Claire had to go to Lutheran Medical Center. In March, she had received a letter from Lutheran's Patient Accounts Department. Her mother's Medicaid application had been returned by the Human Resources Administration's Medical Assistance Program. Someone there had looked at the bankbook Claire submitted to Haydee Santana in January and had wanted an explanation for several "large deposits & large withdrawals" that Mrs. Quinton had made in her savings account between 1979 and 1982. Most of the transactions queried were withdrawals. Kate and Claire Quinton were unable to live the way they wanted to live on their joint income of about $750 a month. Claire had periodically taken money out of her mother's savings account and deposited it in their joint checking account to pay their bills — food, notions, utilities, Claire's Blue Cross and Blue Shield, life insurance, and car insurance. The major transaction queried was a deposit of $2300 that Claire had made in her mother's savings account on January 18, three days before she had started her mother's Medicaid application. Claire telephoned Haydee Santana, who told her to bring in some canceled checks for things like the insurance and the utilities to explain the withdrawals, and a notarized letter to explain the $2300 deposit. Miss Santana wasn't in when Claire went to Lutheran, so Claire gave the canceled checks and the letter to one of her colleagues. According to Claire's letter, the $2300 deposit was her mother's share of a joint certificate of deposit that had recently matured. Claire wrote that she had reinvested her share of the certificate but had put her mother's share in her savings account in case it should be needed to pay for her mother's medical expenses — Dr. Ruffolo's bill of $2100, for example — or, as she said she had feared at the time, for her mother's funeral expenses.

In April, while Mrs. Quinton's Medicaid application was still pending, Cindy Strong and Diane Confalone spoke with the Quintons about their long-range plans. The Quintons' wish was to continue to have Mrs. Quinton live at home with a home attendant provided by the Human Resources Administration, which would take over from Transitional Community Placement as soon as Mrs. Quinton's Medicaid application was approved. On April 14, Miss Strong filled out a Form M-11q, which was a physician's request to the Human Resources Administration for home-care services, and she had Dr. Ruffolo sign it on April 15. An M-11q contains information about a person's diagnoses, medication, impairments, and physical limitations. Cindy Strong wrote on the M-11q that Mrs. Quinton needed assistance fifty-six hours a week. On Monday, April 26, Diane Confalone and David Gould delivered Mrs. Quinton's M-11q to a General Social Services district office in Brooklyn. General Social Services (G.S.S.) is the department of the Human Resources Administration that recommends, among other things, how much home-attendant care an applicant should receive. There are forty-three G.S.S. district offices in New York City. The G.S.S. district office Miss Confalone and Mr. Gould visited handled a thousand home-attendant cases, in several neighborhoods of Brooklyn, including Windsor Terrace. They took Mrs. Quinton's M-11q to the district office, instead of mailing it, because she was the first person on T.C.P. who lived in that jurisdiction. They wanted to meet the director of the office, Seymour Goldsmith, to tell him about T.C.P. They spent a cordial hour and a half with him. In April of 1982, Seymour Goldsmith had a staff of twenty-two, including five supervisors and eleven case managers; each of the case managers handled about ninety cases.

According to H.R.A. procedure, a G.S.S. case manager is supposed to visit an applicant for home care within seventy-two hours of receiving Form M-11q. Within twelve working days, the case manager is supposed to fill out a number of forms and send these forms and the M-11q to the Office of Home Care Services, a division of H.R.A.'s Family and Adult Services, which is situated on East Sixteenth Street, in Manhattan. The Office of Home Care Services reviews the applications submitted by the G.S.S. district offices and authorizes the number of hours of service that the applicant will receive. The most important form that the case manager fills out is an eight-page form called an M-11s. (Of the numbering and lettering of

H.R.A. forms there is no end.) On the M-11s, the case manager must list the tasks that have to be done for the applicant, and the "significant adults" living in the home and those not in the home who can assist with these tasks. The case manager must write a narrative account of the applicant's situation and must recommend the number of hours of home care the client needs. According to state law, H.R.A. must make a decision on an application within thirty days of receiving it.

Mrs. Quinton's application got off to a slow start. Her M-11q was logged in at the district office on April 28. On April 30, it was assigned to Ida Winkel, one of the eleven case managers. Mrs. Winkel telephoned Claire Quinton on May 6 and made an appointment to visit Mrs. Quinton on the afternoon of Friday, May 7. She said she would be driving from her office to 292 Seeley Street. Claire asked her if she would like directions. "I already know the area, but you might as well give me directions," Mrs. Winkel said. Claire told her which avenue to take from her office to reach another main artery and where to make a left turn to get to Seeley Street. "You can't make a left there," Mrs. Winkel said.

Claire was on the verge of saying, "You could twenty minutes ago," but said, "All right, you come your own way. Make a left wherever it suits you."

Mrs. Winkel did not show up at the Quintons', or call them, on the seventh. Claire telephoned her on Monday the tenth to ask what had happened. Mrs. Winkel said she would be there that afternoon at two.

Ida Winkel, a tall woman in her early sixties, who was fashionably dressed in a pink pants suit and a pale-pink blouse, with pale-pink lipstick and nail polish, climbed the stairs to the Quintons' apartment on the afternoon of the tenth. As Claire and Kate Quinton later recalled the visit, Claire showed Mrs. Winkel around and then offered her a chair at the dinette table, where Mrs. Quinton was sitting in her wheelchair chatting with Felicity. "This is a lovely apartment," Mrs. Winkel said. "How much rent do you pay?"

By May, Claire had told her mother about the rent increase of September 1981. "Three hundred and forty-five dollars a month," she answered.

"How does your mother get downstairs?" Mrs. Winkel inquired.

"She doesn't, Mrs. Winkel," Claire answered.

"You and your mother should get out of here and move into a three-room apartment in an elevator building," Mrs. Winkel said.

"I don't know of any apartments available in an elevator building in Windsor Terrace," Claire said. "Apartments of any kind are hard to find in this neighborhood. Why do you think we should move?"

"So that your mother can go outside and sit in the sun."

"My mother is allergic to the sun, Mrs. Winkel. She's been to many dermatologists. One of them told her years ago that whenever she went out she should walk on the shady side of the street."

Mrs. Winkel commented that Claire had a dry cough.

Claire said she had been seeing a doctor about the cough.

"If I were you, Miss Quinton, I'd go to another doctor,"

Mrs. Winkel said. She then asked Mrs. Quinton about her arthritis and her limitations.

Mrs. Quinton told her that the ball of her left foot was the size of a walnut and that she spent almost all her time in bed or in her wheelchair. She said that in the morning Felicity helped her out of bed and into the wheelchair. During the day, Felicity transferred her from the wheelchair to the commode. Mrs. Winkel asked Mrs. Quinton how often she had been transferred from the wheelchair to the commode that day. "I think seven times," Mrs. Quinton said, explaining that she was taking diuretics for her edema. "Ten times," Felicity corrected her. Mrs. Winkel had a few more questions for Felicity about her chores. Mrs. Quinton said she lived for the visits of the physical therapist, who had her using a walker. She said she could walk a few steps but hoped she would be able to walk better when her Medicaid application was approved and she could order the special molded shoes he had told her she needed. With a walker, she would again be able to go to the toilet; the wheelchair wouldn't go through the door to the bathroom. Mrs. Winkel asked the Quintons about the status of Mrs. Quinton's Medicaid application, about the T.C.P. program and what it provided, and about other close relatives who might be able to help care for Mrs. Quinton. Claire gave Mrs. Winkel the names and addresses of Barbara and of Mrs. Quinton's two sisters — Eileen, who lived in Brooklyn, and Sheila, who lived in Connecticut. She said that Barbara was unwilling to help, that Eileen couldn't help, because she was seventy-three and suffered from arthritis, and that Sheila couldn't help, because she was seventy-nine

and suffered from asthma. Mrs. Winkel asked Kate and
Claire Quinton how they had managed before T.C.P.
Claire told her that her mother had had a home-care
worker from Selfhelp who had come in about twice a
week for two hours in 1981, before and after her breast
operation, and that a nurse from Nursing Sisters had made
periodic visits. She also said that her mother had had a
physical therapist in 1981, just as she did in 1982.

"If you could manage with four hours a week of home
care last year, why do you need someone fifty-six hours
a week now?" Mrs. Winkel asked.

Claire said that her mother's poor condition in the
spring of 1981 had taken a terrible toll, because the hours
of help her mother was receiving then were insufficient.
She said that in the summer of 1981, after the breast
operation, her mother had been able to get right back
on the walker. Claire said she believed that it would be
more difficult for her mother to get back on her feet in
1982. "If a young woman stays in bed for two months,
she'll be weaker when she gets up, but when a woman
of seventy-nine or eighty is in bed that long it's much
harder for her to bounce back," she said. In a soft voice,
so that her mother wouldn't hear her, Claire said, "My
mother is slowly withering away, Mrs. Winkel. There
were long periods in 1981 when she wouldn't eat, and
she went into the hospital this year with malnutrition.
I could plot her decline on a graph."

After filling in sections of several forms and scribbling
notes on several pieces of scratch paper, Mrs. Winkel
said she was ready to leave. She told Claire she wanted
to call her office. "It's a funny thing," she said. "The

office phone number was changed a couple of months ago. I still can't remember the new number and I don't have it with me." When Claire offered to give Mrs. Winkel the number of her office, she said she had changed her mind about calling. She said she had decided to visit another client who lived a couple of blocks from Seeley Street. First, she said she wanted to look up the client's telephone number in the Brooklyn directory. Then she said she had changed her mind: she wouldn't telephone, she would just drop in. In the foyer, she asked Claire if she had any clout at H.R.A. Claire said that she did. "Who is he?" Mrs. Winkel asked. Claire's cousin Douglas, her aunt Sheila's son, had a good friend who was a high-ranking H.R.A. official. Claire had asked Douglas to call his friend to see if he could expedite her mother's Medicaid application. Claire named the man for Mrs. Winkel.

"How do you spell that?" Mrs. Winkel asked. Claire spelled the man's name. Mrs. Winkel put her right foot on the first stair step and spun around. "Oh, by the way, Miss Quinton, what do you do for a living?" she asked. Claire said that when she was able to work she had been a secretary, and that she had been unable to work since 1976 and had applied for and had been awarded disability. She said she had had five spinal fusions of lumbars four and five, and that she suffered from depression. Mrs. Winkel asked her for the name of the lawyer who had represented her at the disability hearing, for the name of the presiding judge, and for the name of the psychiatrist she had been seeing. Mrs. Winkel then asked Claire how many years of education she had had. Claire told her that she had completed about a year and a half of college. "You should go back to work as a secretary," Mrs. Winkel said. "There are plenty of jobs available on Thirteenth Avenue." Claire said she hoped to return to work when she felt better and her mother was more self-sufficient. If Mrs. Quinton could use a walker, Claire could leave the house without worrying about her mother's safety when home attendants didn't show up.

Most of the jobs that Claire had had in the 1950s and 1960s were in office buildings in the Wall Street area. She didn't want to work on Thirteenth Avenue, a shabby place lined with discount stores, fish markets, pizza parlors, and delicatessens. The sidewalks were peopled by peddlers. It seemed imprudent to tell Mrs. Winkel that there were no tall office buildings on Thirteenth Avenue. It troubled Claire that six years had gone by since she had last worked. She often worried that she would never be able to work again, regardless of her mother's condition.

On the morning of Monday, May 17, when Kate Quinton's application for home care should have been on its way to the Office of Home Care Services, Mrs. Winkel telephoned Claire. Her tone the previous Monday had been crisp and curt. This time, Claire felt, she sounded extremely annoyed. She immediately asked Claire how Mrs. Quinton's grocery shopping was done. Claire said she bought the *News* on Sunday, clipped the cents-off coupons from the paper, and studied the food ads to look for sales and specials. A friend usually drove her to a supermarket on Sunday after church. She read the food ads in the *News* again on Wednesday, when additional specials were often advertised, and usually shopped again that afternoon. Wednesday at two o'clock was a good time to shop at one particular supermarket, because on Wednesdays the boys from a nearby parochial school got out at one o'clock. They hung around the supermarket and carried groceries from the checkout counter to the car for a quarter. Felicity carried the groceries upstairs. Claire said she sometimes went to a fish market on Friday to buy fresh fish. Mrs. Winkel asked Claire if Felicity did any shopping. Claire said she occasionally asked Felicity to pick up a loaf of bread or another item or two when she went out for her lunch at the Burger King. She didn't want to tell Mrs. Winkel in front of Felicity, who was close enough to the telephone to hear what Claire was saying, that she didn't ask Felicity to do much shopping because she often got things wrong. Once, Claire had asked her to buy a bottle of Lemon Fresh Joy, a dishwashing liquid; Felicity had returned with a bottle of lemon juice. Mrs. Quinton was accustomed to writing out succinct grocery lists for Claire, of items like "milk" or "chicken." If Claire forgot to rewrite the lists for Felicity, spelling out exactly what to buy, Felicity was apt to return with a whole chicken instead of the quartered chicken Mrs. Quinton wanted. If the list said just "milk," Felicity might buy a quart of whole milk when Mrs. Quinton wanted a half-gallon of ninety-nine-percent-fatfree milk. Claire's account of the Quintons' shopping habits seemed to infuriate Mrs. Winkel. "I know people who can shop for a family of six once a week," she shouted.

"That's well and good, Mrs. Winkel, but my mother and I have never shopped that way, and I like to shop for the sales," Claire replied. Claire was upset by Mrs.

Winkel's tone and by her shouting. She didn't want to raise her own voice, so she hung up. She telephoned the G.S.S. district office and asked to speak to Mrs. Winkel's superior. Seymour Goldsmith got on the phone. Claire told him that Mrs. Winkel had given her a bad time. She said she thought it was none of Mrs. Winkel's business to tell people who lived in four rooms that they ought to live in three. Mr. Goldsmith told Claire he was writing down what she said, and asked the senior supervisor in the office, Jacqueline Laroche, to call Claire Quinton. Claire repeated to Mrs. Laroche what she had already said to Seymour Goldsmith, added some details, and said that she had found Mrs. Winkel arrogant and verbally abusive.

CHAPTER FOUR

S HORTLY AFTER MRS. WINKEL HAD annoyed Claire
Quinton on May 10 by telling her how to live her life
("If I were you, Miss Quinton, I'd go to another doctor. . . . You should go back to work as a secretary"),
Claire saw Barbara for the first time since January 20,
when Barbara had exasperated her by telling her, as was
her custom, how to live her life ("Get yourself together,
Claire. . . . Lose weight. Get a job. And get someone in
to share the expenses of the apartment"). On May 10,
Felicity had washed Mrs. Quinton's hair. Mrs. Quinton
had put it up in pins and left the pins in until the fourteenth, so that her hair would last the weekend. (The
permanent that Felicity's friend had given her hadn't
taken.) On Saturday, May 15, Kate Quinton's grand-
daughter Sarah was getting married to Brian in Teaneck.
She had been looking forward to the wedding for months.
On her eightieth birthday, Sarah had said to her in the

hospital, "Grandma, you're not going to miss out on my wedding even if I have to drive in and get you myself."

Claire was not looking forward to the trip to Teaneck, but she was eager to see her nephew and nieces — she hadn't seen Charles for two years, and she hadn't seen Sarah and Elizabeth for about six months. She felt close to the children, because Barbara and Dwight had still been living with Kate and Claire Quinton, in a house that Mrs. Quinton had owned in Brooklyn, when their first two children were born. Claire had done a lot of babysitting for Charles and Sarah. The four Gaylords had moved to Teaneck before Elizabeth was born, but Claire had spent time at their house in Teaneck recuperating after her spinal fusions, in 1960, 1964, 1965, 1968, and 1969. She had taught Charles how to play backgammon and had watched endless hours of Saturday-morning television cartoons with Sarah and Elizabeth. Claire dreaded Sarah's wedding, however, because she didn't want to see Dwight or Barbara. Neither she nor her mother had spoken to Dwight since February, when Dwight told Claire her mother was a bitch. Barbara usually telephoned Mrs. Quinton when she thought that Claire would be at church. If Barbara called when Claire was home and Claire answered, Barbara said, "May I please speak to my mother?" and Claire handed her mother the phone. In April, when Claire's invitation to Sarah's wedding came in the mail, she telephoned Sarah and asked to be seated at a table as far away as possible from her sister and brother-in-law at the reception.

On Thursday, May 6, Barbara had telephoned her mother to tell her that she was arranging to have Brian's brother and brother-in-law pick her and Claire up and drive them to the home of Donald and Betty Healy, in Teaneck, where they would spend Friday and Saturday night. Mrs. Quinton and Claire knew the Healys. Mrs. Quinton had bought a house in Teaneck in 1972, and she and Claire had lived there until December of 1975. Barbara said she would call soon with more details. She didn't call on Friday, Saturday, Sunday, or Monday. Mrs. Quinton was fretful. She liked to know her precise plans well in advance. When Barbara called on Tuesday evening, the eleventh, she told her mother that Brian's brother and brother-in-law would fetch her and Claire on the afternoon of the fourteenth, between three and four. She said that on Friday, before the rehearsal dinner got under way, Mrs. Quinton and Claire would come to her house to have a light dinner with Glenda and Liam, Mrs. Quinton's two great-grandchildren.

Claire was sitting at the dinette table when Barbara called. Barbara's voice is loud, and Claire heard every word she said. She took the phone out of her mother's hands. "Barbara, you must be a little bit out of your mind," she said. "After all that happened in the last few months, I'm never going to take another crumb from you, and I'm never going to set foot in your house again. All I want is a ride to church in Teaneck on Sunday morning with Elizabeth."

Early on Friday, Mrs. Quinton unpinned her hair, and Claire went to the dry cleaner's to fetch the clothes she and her mother were going to wear to the wedding. The dry cleaner had promised to have them ready on Thursday night. They weren't ready on Friday morning. He told Claire to return in an hour. Shortly after she got home, at ten-forty-five, the telephone rang. It was Brian's sister Julia calling to say that her husband and her brother would be there in about half an hour or forty-five minutes. Claire told Julia that she couldn't be ready that soon because the dry cleaner had let her down. She didn't want the two young men to have to wait, and suggested that they come at twelve-fifteen. They agreed to. In spite of all the fretting about plans, Mrs. Quinton had a good time seeing her great-grandchildren that evening, and Claire had a quiet time at the Healys'.

On Saturday morning, Claire helped her mother put on a becoming print dress and jacket, a string of black beads, and a pair of open-toed shoes. The day was warm but not humid, and Mrs. Quinton's hair stayed up. An usher pushed her wheelchair up the aisle of the church and parked it adjacent to the first pew on the bride's side, where Barbara and Dwight were seated. Claire wore a powder-blue suit that complemented her eyes. She was escorted to the second pew and sat with her aunt Eileen and her friend Helen Durbin. Charles's wife, Jessica, and their two children, and Jessica's mother, Noreen, were in the third pew. During the wedding Mass, when the priest said, "Now let us turn and give each other the sign of peace," Claire shook hands with Helen and Eileen and quickly turned to the third pew. Jessica, Glenda, and Liam kissed Claire, and Claire shook hands with Noreen, who was out of kissing reach. "I'm not going to be a hypocrite and shake hands with Barbara and Dwight," she later recalled thinking as she avoided the first pew.

Dwight Gaylord pushed Mrs. Quinton's wheelchair up

the aisle after the ceremony. She and Eileen sat at Barbara and Dwight's table at the reception. Mrs. Quinton made small talk with Barbara. She didn't speak to Dwight. So many people came up to her to tell her how well she looked that she felt, she said, like a queen. Claire's table of ten was congenial. Two people who realized that Claire had kept her mother out of a nursing home complimented her on her mother's appearance, and a third said to her, "I know what you're going through. Let me know if ever you need help."

On Sunday morning, Barbara telephoned the Healys' house. Betty Healy answered the telephone. Barbara told her that Elizabeth would be over to fetch Mrs. Quinton and Claire at eleven to drive them back to Brooklyn, because she had to take some people to the airport in the afternoon. Donald Healy followed Elizabeth's car to the Quintons', to help lift Mrs. Quinton. They carried her up the stairs. After Mrs. Quinton was settled in the kitchen, Claire walked to church.

A few days later, Claire went to see her therapist, Irene Garcia, who knew how anxious she had been about the wedding.

"How did it go?" she asked Claire.

"It bothered the hell out of me," Claire said. "I can't believe my sister. She's unreal. Sweetheart in Teaneck can gloss over all the trouble in the family between January and April and act as if everything were a bed of roses in May."

Irene told Claire to scream if she thought that would help get the rage out of her system. Claire didn't scream, but she cried, and then she talked. She told Irene how much she resented Barbara for keeping her mother cliff-hanging from Thursday to Tuesday about the precise plans to get to the wedding and for denying her the one favor she had asked — a ride to church — with the transparently phony excuse that Elizabeth had to go to the airport. She said it troubled her that her mother had been upset between Barbara's telephone calls but had later refused to admit her feelings. Irene reminded Claire that she knew her mother had blinders on as far as Barbara was concerned, and that deep down Claire cared for her sister and would help Barbara if she were in adversity. Claire agreed that she didn't wish Barbara any misfortune, but she said firmly that she didn't need the "aggravation" that Barbara caused her every time she saw her. "Fine, stay away from her," Irene said. "You want to avoid trouble, and that's a very healthy thing to do."

❧

A few days before the wedding, Claire Quinton had notified Louisa Dyson, the Family Home Care case coordinator who had taken over the T.C.P. cases from Evelyn Partisi in late April, that her mother would be away the weekend of May 15 and 16, and therefore wouldn't need Belinda that Saturday and Sunday. Belinda Fernández worked for Mrs. Quinton for two more weekends. When she left on May 30, she didn't tell the Quintons that that was the last day she would see them. Diane Confalone called Claire later to tell her that Belinda would not be coming back. She didn't tell her precisely why. Mrs. Cooper and Belinda had been on very friendly terms. Olivia Cooper felt as if they were partners in a good cause: caring for Gerald Cooper. As the weeks passed, however, Mrs. Cooper apparently had begun to realize how much she and her husband depended on Belinda. She began to act resentful. She behaved as if she were afraid of becoming too dependent on Belinda herself. She stopped taking her daily nap and wouldn't let Belinda fix her lunch. She turned cold to Belinda, who was hurt by the change in her attitude. Belinda also found the Quintons too "picky." She decided that being a home attendant was too stressful. She told Diane Confalone that she would stay with the Coopers only until the end of the month, until they could find another home attendant. She eventually returned to work in a garment factory.

The month of June began inauspiciously for Mrs. Quinton. On June 2, she got a urinary-tract infection. Claire made a number of telephone calls and found a urologist who would come to the house; he prescribed medication to treat the infection. On June 3, Mrs. Quinton's joints ached so much that she couldn't do her leg exercises. For the weekend of June 5 and 6, Louisa Dyson had assigned Mrs. Quinton a temporary weekend home attendant named Cecille DuFief, a Haitian immigrant who was studying nursing. Mrs. Quinton found her slovenly and inefficient; Miss DuFief spent a good part of the weekend sleeping in a chair. The following weekend, Mrs. Dyson sent Mrs. Quinton Cecille DuFief's sister Jeanne, who was also taking a nursing course. Jeanne DuFief brought some needlepoint work with her. Whenever Mrs. Quinton asked her for something, Jeanne said,

"In a minute." Mrs. Quinton waited seven or eight minutes each time she had to use the commode. Then Louisa Dyson assigned Mrs. Quinton a permanent weekend home attendant, a Haitian woman named Dominique Jaqua, who was supposed to arrive at the Quintons' at ten o'clock on Saturday, June 19. At eleven, she telephoned and said she was lost. Claire told her how to find the house. Mrs. Jaqua appeared at eleven-thirty wearing four-inch-high stiletto heels and a party dress. Claire called Family Home Care's emergency number and spoke to the woman who answered about Dominique Jaqua's lateness and inappropriate apparel. The woman asked to speak to Mrs. Jaqua. She informed her that she had been late and was improperly dressed, and asked if she wanted to stay. She said she didn't. The woman told Claire she would send Mrs. Quinton another home attendant on Sunday. Dominique Jaqua left at twelve-fifty. Later that afternoon, Claire received two threatening telephone calls. The voice at the other end of the line sounded like Dominique Jaqua's.

Zenobia Nelson, who came to the Quintons' on the twentieth, was a considerate, middle-aged American who had a full-time job in a nursing home. She worked as a home attendant on her days off. She was one of only six "on call" weekend home attendants that Family Home Care employed for its 1150 clients. Louisa Dyson had made a home visit to the Quintons' and had liked Kate and Claire. She thought she had found a good home attendant for Mrs. Quinton for the weekend of June 26 and 27, and called Claire to say she was sending a home attendant who had wonderful experience. This home attendant called Mrs. Dyson on Friday afternoon to say she couldn't work that weekend. Louisa Dyson picked another person — Martine Latour — out of the Cardex of a colleague, called her, and assigned her to the Quintons. Martine Latour didn't know how to empty a commode. When she made Mrs. Quinton's bed, she put her afghan between the bottom sheet and the top sheet. On Monday the twenty-eighth, when Claire telephoned Louisa Dyson to complain about Miss Latour, she learned that the woman who had worked at the Quintons' that weekend and who had answered to the name Martine was a woman named Élise Gentil. Miss Latour had worked on another case that weekend. Her roommate, Élise, had answered the telephone when Louisa Dyson had called on Friday, and had taken the job. "It's difficult to get good home attendants on weekends, and summer weekends are especially difficult," Mrs. Dyson said. "The majority of home attendants in New York City are foreign-born, and most of them are from the West Indies. In June, they start leaving for the islands."

Kate Quinton's Medicaid application had been approved in May. Dr. Beyer was in the process of moving from Brooklyn to Long Island, and Claire spent several weeks tracking him down. He wrote out a prescription for Kate Quinton's molded shoes on June 18. On June 23, Evan Flint told Mrs. Quinton he would not visit her again until she had the molded shoes. Nursing Sisters Home Visiting Service is reimbursed by Medicare for short-term acute care or rehabilitative care. Once a person's condition is stabilized, as Kate Quinton's had been, the person is considered a chronic case, and Medicare will no longer pay for services such as physical therapy.

Claire Quinton's back had become worse in late June. She went to see an orthopedic surgeon. He recommended that she have a CAT scan of the body. Claire had the CAT scan at Lutheran on June 28. The orthopedic surgeon told her it showed that she had a degenerative disc between the third and fourth lumbars and might require another operation.

The month of June ended as inauspiciously for the Quintons as it had begun. It was probably fortunate that they had only an inkling of what was happening at the G.S.S. district office with Kate Quinton's application for a home attendant. When Ida Winkel had asked Claire if she had any clout at H.R.A., Claire had thought Mrs. Winkel meant that clout was useful for getting on Medicaid. She had no idea that Ida Winkel was planning to do her best to cut back on the number of hours of home care her mother had been receiving.

🦢

Not long after Claire Quinton hung up on Mrs. Winkel on May 17, Ida Winkel telephoned Cindy Strong. She told her she didn't believe Kate Quinton needed a home attendant fifty-six hours a week; something like thirty-five hours a week would be more than sufficient. Claire Quinton appeared capable to Mrs. Winkel, and as she wasn't working Mrs. Winkel thought she could do more for her mother than she was doing. Cindy Strong had decided in late February that Mrs. Quinton required a home attendant fifty-six hours a week. Nothing she had seen since had made her change her mind. Although Cindy Strong was about to leave T.C.P. — she was moving from Brooklyn to New Jersey and had found a new job there — she wanted Mrs. Quinton to be able to stay at home. She didn't like having her nursing judgment questioned, and Mrs. Winkel struck her as obnoxious. She was furious, and went to David Gould to tell him about Mrs. Winkel's call.

David Gould telephoned Ida Winkel on Friday, May 21. He said he agreed with Miss Strong's professional judgment, and inquired, diplomatically, what he could do to move Mrs. Quinton's application along. Ida Winkel bombarded David Gould with questions. What was City Planning doing in the field of home health care? Why didn't City Planning stick to issues like housing and zoning? Why should she have to take any recommendations from T.C.P.? Before Mr. Gould could answer any of Mrs. Winkel's questions, she interrupted him. "Mrs. Winkel, you'll have to be quiet and let me finish my sentences," he said. He also indicated that the application should have been processed long ago.

"Why don't you just get us more case managers, so that we won't be so overworked?" Ida Winkel asked.

"I wish I had such power, Mrs. Winkel," he answered. "There's no point in continuing this conversation, so won't you please process the application?"

On Monday, May 24, Seymour Goldsmith, Mrs. Winkel's superior, telephoned David Gould. He acknowledged that there was a problem with the processing of Kate Quinton's application, and said that he would let David Gould know when it had been solved.

On June 1, David Gould received a call from Jacque-

line Laroche. Mrs. Laroche told him that she disagreed
with Ida Winkel's assessment of Kate and Claire Quinton.
She had been aware of the case since May 17, when she
spoke to Claire. Mrs. Winkel had been stalling; she had
asked Mrs. Laroche why she should have to make two
evaluations of Mrs. Quinton's needs — one before she got
her molded shoes and one afterward. Jacqueline Laroche
told David Gould that she had had some prior bad ex-
periences with Ida Winkel and had therefore wanted to
proceed cautiously. She was finally taking the case into
her own hands, she said, because she was going to be
out of the office on jury duty for a week, starting June 7,
and wanted the application on its way to the Office of
Home Care Services before her return. In her opinion,
Kate Quinton needed fifty-six hours of home-attendant
care. She was afraid that because Mrs. Quinton's primary
diagnosis was gallbladder disease and her secondary diagnosis was severe osteoarthritis she might not get the fifty-
six hours without some additional proof of need. She
asked David Gould to send her Kate Quinton's latest
DMS-1 score. He did so. It was 250 — still skilled-nursing-
care level. Mrs. Laroche said she would call Claire Quinton to request evidence of her inability to care for her
mother. Mr. Gould telephoned Claire to ask her to cooper-
ate with Jacqueline Laroche. Mrs. Laroche called Claire
and explained the situation. Claire photostated a copy of
a letter that an orthopedic surgeon had written for her
in the fall of 1977, when she was applying for disability
benefits. The letter described Claire's back problems and
mentioned her broken ankle, which had not healed properly. Claire told Mrs. Laroche she would get a letter from

her psychiatrist; he wrote to the district office promptly on her behalf. Mrs. Laroche also telephoned Nursing Sisters Home Visiting Service. The social worker who had been assigned to the Quintons in April of 1981 and had helped them over a crisis that spring wrote to Mrs. Laroche. "It is our belief that Mrs. Quinton requires an attendant for eight hours per day, seven days a week, to allow her to improve her functioning, to prevent further deterioration in her condition, and to allow for supervised physical activity on a daily basis as recommended by our physical therapist," the social worker's letter read. "We further believe that the patient's daughter is not capable of providing the care needed by the patient because of her own physical and psychiatric limitations."

On June 9, Seymour Goldsmith called David Gould to say that the district office would be sending Kate Quinton's application to the Office of Home Care Services in a day or two. He told him that because of the disagreement within the district office the application would be directed to O.H.C.S.'s Division of Medical Review (most applications were simply sent to O.H.C.S.), with Mrs. Laroche's recommendation of fifty-six hours and the data she had gathered, along with Ida Winkel's recommendation of thirty-five hours and her M-11s form.

On June 23, David Gould had lunch with an old acquaintance, the head of H.R.A.'s Family and Adult Services. He told him he had a problem case, and asked what to do about it. Eight and a half weeks had gone by since Kate Quinton's M-11q had been delivered to the G.S.S. district office, and Kate Quinton had now been on T.C.P. for over three and a half months. The acquaintance referred him to his deputy at Family and Adult Services. David Gould called her on the twenty-fourth. She called him back on the twenty-fifth to say that the Division of Medical Review had agreed with Mrs. Laroche and had authorized fifty-six hours a week of home-attendant care for Kate Quinton.

Even after Mrs. Quinton's application was sent to O.H.C.S., Ida Winkel kept trying to defend her point of view. She telephoned Diane Confalone on June 18. The call was essentially a repeat performance of her May 21 conversation with David Gould. After twenty-five minutes, Miss Confalone told Mrs. Winkel to speak to Mr. Goldsmith if she had any further questions. "It's obvious that you don't want to talk to me," Ida Winkel said. Diane Confalone said that that was correct. Even after O.H.C.S. granted Mrs. Quinton a home attendant for fifty-six hours a week, Mrs. Winkel continued to attempt to justify her position. She kept a curiously inaccurate record of the case on a form that stayed at the district office. In her last entry, dated July 26, 1982, Mrs. Winkel wrote that David Gould had agreed that six hours a day of home care would be adequate for Kate Quinton — something he had never done.

On July 28, Ida Winkel fell out of a chair in the district office and went on sick leave. Her supervisors, who had given her a poor evaluation as a case manager, found it ironic that she had been screaming at a home attendant when she fell. The home attendant was taking care of two elderly sisters who were terminally ill with lung cancer. The sisters were spinsters; one was blind, the other threw up most of the night. The home attendant slept on a bed between them. She was working twenty-four hours a day but getting paid for only twelve hours. (In December of 1982, H.R.A. had 4721 home-attendant cases it called "twenty-four-hour sleep-in" cases, in which the home attendant was there twenty-four hours but was paid for only twelve hours of work; it had just 384 "twenty-four-hour split shift" cases, for which two home attendants were paid for working twelve hours apiece.) The home attendant had come in to the district office to tell Mrs. Winkel that the case was more than she could bear, and Ida Winkel was shouting at her because she didn't think that the attendant was handling the case well.

The case wouldn't have existed if it had not been for Ida Winkel. One sister had been in a hospital, and the hospital had planned to send her to a hospice. When Mrs. Winkel learned of this plan, she had intervened and had the woman sent home, so that one home attendant could care for both women, thereby saving the taxpayers' money. As soon as Mrs. Winkel went on sick leave, Jacqueline Laroche got in touch with O.H.C.S.; within one day, the case was on a twenty-four-hour split shift. Several years earlier, Ida Winkel had put through an application recommending that a family be given a home attendant for half an hour a day seven days a week. Mrs. Laroche had taken the case away from her. Over the years, Jacqueline Laroche had tried to understand Ida Winkel and to counsel her. She knew that Mrs. Winkel perceived herself as a dedicated woman who was doing her job by saving the taxpayers' money, by encouraging relatives to do as much as possible for clients, and by dissuading clients from becoming dependent on home attendants.

Ida Winkel had made many sacrifices in taking care of her aged father and father-in-law, and of her husband before his death; she believed that others should make similar sacrifices. When Jacqueline Laroche told her, "You can't save money at the expense of human beings" — according to one colleague, several people to whom Ida Winkel denied sufficient care had died in misery — the words had made no impression on her.

Seymour Goldsmith expected Ida Winkel to return to work and waited until fall to redistribute her cases among the ten other case managers. When they took over, many of them told Mr. Goldsmith that Mrs. Winkel's cases were characterized by her "unwillingness to give." Many of them also found that Ida Winkel's clients were intimidated. When the case managers offered to increase home-attendant hours, the clients hesitated to accept, fearing that Mrs. Winkel would seek revenge after she returned. Ida Winkel successfully applied for workmen's compensation. She has since retired and moved to California.

Seymour Goldsmith does not like to find himself in the position of defending Ida Winkel. He claims that H.R.A.'s philosophy is "If we must err, let us err on the side of leniency." He does, however, acknowledge the rapid increase in the size of the home-attendant caseload in recent years and says that the authorization of hours of service to clients is the one area in which H.R.A. has some ability to try to hold back the equally rapid rise in cost. In December of 1978, there were 11,900 H.R.A. home-attendant cases in New York City. In December of 1982, there were 26,443 cases. In fiscal year 1977, home-attendant care cost

$69.2 million; in fiscal year 1982 it cost $279.34 million. Of this $279.34 million, approximately twenty-five percent was paid by New York City, approximately twenty-five percent was paid by New York State, and approximately fifty percent was paid by the federal government. In December of 1982, H.R.A. paid on the average for 51.4 hours per week per home-attendant client. The hourly cost of this care was $4.85: $3.35 per hour to the home attendant in salary, $1.06 an hour for fringe benefits, and $.44 an hour to the vendor agency for administrative overhead. The yearly cost of the 51.4 hours a week of home-attendant care was $12,963. In December of 1982, the average annual cost of keeping a patient in a skilled nursing home in New York City was $29,500.

Critics of home care say that comparing the cost of nursing-home care with the cost of home care is deceptive, because home care requires additional expenditures for things like food, rent, and utilities, on top of the cost of home-attendant services; they don't see the two as an either/or proposition. They believe that home care is an "add on" cost, and contend that if it weren't available, or were more limited, families would not necessarily put their elderly in nursing homes but would make sacrifices (as Ida Winkel did and would have others do) to keep them at home. Many H.R.A. officials dispute this, and point to people like Kate Quinton, who would have gone to a nursing home if Claire had been unable to obtain adequate home-attendant care. These officials say that there is also an unfair double standard. If a person qualifies for Medicaid and is accepted by a nursing home, Medicaid covers the costs and expects nothing of the person's children. If the children choose to keep the person at home, thereby saving Medicaid thousands of dollars, they bear a great deal of the burden. The officials say that home attendants supplement rather than supplant relatives.

In fiscal 1982, New York State spent seventy-eight percent of all the Medicaid dollars spent on home health care in the United States. Seventy-three percent of the state's Medicaid home-care cases were in New York City. In early 1983, the number of home-attendant cases was increasing by about 271 a month. The larger caseload was not the only reason for the rise in costs, however. Many home attendants have become unionized, and unions have begun to exact a wage increase of thirty cents an hour from most vendor agencies for home attendants who have had more than 2100 hours of work experience. The rapid increase in the caseload is attributable to such factors as the larger Medicaid-eligible population; the shortage of nursing homes in New York City; more widespread knowledge of H.R.A.'s Home Attendant Program; the increasing percentage of New York City's population that is elderly (many of the elderly live alone); and a growing emphasis on deinstitutionalization. In his first State of the State message, in January of 1983, Governor Mario Cuomo said, "I shall support programs that encourage in-home care for the elderly among families and friends, that avoid their often inappropriate placement in nursing homes."

⁂

The Office of Home Care Services' Vendor Assignment Unit did not notify Family Home Care Services of Brooklyn and Queens that Kate Quinton had become one of its 1150 H.R.A. clients until July 6, so she remained on T.C.P. in June. One day in late June, Diane Confalone learned that Mrs. Quinton had again been accepted by Cobble Hill; it was her obligation to call Mrs. Quinton with the news. By then, Kate Quinton knew more about Cobble Hill than she had known when she hadn't wanted to go there in January. Breakfast was served at seven, lunch at noon, and dinner at five. There was no choice of menus. Of 520 patients at Cobble Hill, only 150 usually were brought down to the dining room; a fair number of them were slumped over in their wheelchairs and talked to themselves rather than to each other. Almost all the patients shared sparsely furnished rooms; they were allowed very few personal possessions. Seventy-five percent of the patients had come to Cobble Hill at the insistence of their families and against their own wishes. As is true in most nursing homes, many patients quickly became depressed. No matter how badly things were going on T.C.P., Mrs. Quinton always told Cindy Strong she never wanted to hear the words "nursing home." Claire had never expressed regret over taking her mother home. Mrs. Quinton declined with alacrity her second opportunity to go to Cobble Hill.

In late June, Claire Quinton found out that Dr. Ruffolo would not accept Medicaid. He later told Diane Confalone that there was too much paperwork involved. Rose Carrese, Cindy Strong's replacement, helped Mrs. Quinton become a patient of Lutheran's Family Physician Service, which is a group of doctors doing a three-year residency in family practice, a specialty recognized by the American Medical Association. A family-practice physician treats all a patient's ailments to the limit of his competence before referring the patient to a specialist, as distinct from the currently more common method of having the patient go directly to a specialist for each ailment. The residents, who are supervised by Lutheran's attending doctors, make home visits, run an outpatient clinic, and admit patients to Lutheran when necessary. T.C.P. had made an arrangement with Family Physician Service to take care of patients on the program who did not have private doctors. One resident, Dr. Louis Romero, was to be Mrs. Quinton's primary doctor, but the other doctors in the service would cover for Dr. Romero when he was not on duty. Family Physician Service charges patients on a sliding scale according to their ability to pay; there is no charge to Medicaid patients. When Rose Carrese and Diane Confalone visited Mrs. Quinton in early July to officially discharge her from T.C.P., she and Claire expressed their gratitude. "Oh, I'll miss you," Mrs. Quinton said. "When I can walk, I would like to make dinner for you."

As far as David Gould and Diane Confalone were concerned, Mrs. Quinton was a successful T.C.P. case. While she was on T.C.P., her DMS-1 score had dropped from 394 to 209. The program had accomplished its main goal, which was to keep her at home until she had Medicaid and could become an H.R.A. client. In early 1983, Diane Confalone and David Gould did a study of the first twenty-four patients discharged from T.C.P. Twelve, in-

cluding Kate Quinton, eventually got Medicaid home-
care services. Of the twelve, one died three months after
leaving T.C.P. — Gerald Cooper. Another, Frances Goya,
had been evicted from her apartment several months
after returning home on T.C.P., and had gone to live with
her adopted daughter. The daughter's husband threat-
ened to kill her. She was rehospitalized, and this time
was discharged from Lutheran to a Health Related Facility. Another patient died on T.C.P. before her Medicaid
application had been processed. Of the first twenty-four
patients, six who were not eligible for Medicaid left the
program with home attendants for whom they paid privately. Two of the six died after leaving T.C.P. One
patient went home on T.C.P. and decided a day later
that she didn't need a home attendant. Another patient
went from T.C.P. to a pilot program that is sponsored
at Lutheran Medical Center by the New York City Department for the Aging. It is a program for people with
Medicare but not Medicaid who don't qualify for Medicare's home-health-care services, and who, in order to
stay at home, need no more than twenty hours a week
of homemaker services. Three others died before T.C.P.
was able to transfer them to long-term care.

T.C.P. has helped unblock beds at Lutheran; patients
have been diverted, at their request, from nursing homes;
and it has cost the taxpayers considerably less money to
have them remain at home than it would have cost to
have them stay on in the hospital and later to maintain
them in a nursing home. By early 1983, T.C.P. had hired
a second nurse and a secretary, and had increased its

original caseload of five patients a month to fourteen patients a month. It had also raised additional private funds and had begun taking patients home from two other hospitals in Brooklyn.

CHAPTER FIVE

IN JULY, KATE AND CLAIRE QUINTON scarcely noticed that Mrs. Quinton was an H.R.A. client rather
than a T.C.P. patient, because they were still getting the
same number of home-attendant hours from the same
vendor agency and because they were so caught up in
their troubles with these home attendants. Felicity Sánchez had started to slack off in June, just as Kate Quinton
was becoming more mobile — at least, in her wheelchair.
After bruising her hands several times going through
doorways, she had learned to give her wheels a good
push and quickly put her hands in her lap while she
glided through the doorway. As she got about more, she
became more aware of Felicity's sloppiness. Felicity put
wet dishes back in the cabinets. Instead of closing the
dresser drawers by using the drawer handles, she pushed
the drawers shut with her hands, leaving fingerprints on
them. She also left fingerprints on the walls. By June,

Mrs. Quinton was able to do some cooking with Felicity's assistance. If she was preparing a stew, Felicity did the things that the arthritis in Kate Quinton's right hand prevented her from doing, such as scraping carrots. Felicity had no aptitude for cooking. She was also arriving late and pleading to leave early.

In June, Felicity told the Quintons that she was about to lose her eight-dollar-a-week babysitter and was having trouble replacing her. She said she would be taking the first two weeks of July off, to go on a vacation. She said she was going to Niagara Falls and Canada with her husband and children. Then she said that she was planning a trip to the Poconos. Then she was off to the Jersey Shore. Her stories about her babysitting situation were similarly varied. Felicity's last day of work before her two-week vacation was July 2. After having five weekend home attendants during the four weekends in June, Claire told Louisa Dyson that her aunt Eileen was visiting over the July 4 weekend and that she would manage without a home attendant then. She knew that July 4 was one of the paid holidays that home attendants receive. Mrs. Dyson promised to send her a permanent weekend home attendant the following weekend. On July 6, Anita LaLuz came to substitute for the vacationing Felicity. Miss LaLuz was an amiable young Puerto Rican woman who was much more skillful than Felicity. She was the first home attendant the Quintons had had since Belinda to wash the kitchen valance. She entertained Mrs. Quinton by telling her about the elaborate plans for her forthcoming wedding. The Quintons were sorry to say goodbye to Anita on July 16. Yolanda Encalada, who had become

Mrs. Quinton's weekend home attendant on July 10, was anything but promising. She was a twenty-two-year-old native of Ecuador who spoke little, hummed a great deal, and cast a cold eye on the commode. "It goes with the job," Claire told her. On the sixteenth, the Quintons made plans to crack down on Felicity when she returned to work on the nineteenth. Kate Quinton hadn't let Anita do some of the chores she had offered to do, because she wanted Felicity to do them. On Monday, she would ask her to clean the oven and the broiler. She would insist that she arrive at ten o'clock in the morning and stay until six o'clock in the evening.

Felicity Sánchez did not show up at ten, at ten-twenty, or even at eleven on Monday, July 19. Claire was upset. A number of times in May and June, when Felicity was not feeling well, Claire had driven her to the babysitter's house and then driven her home. It was one bus ride from the Quintons' house to the babysitter's house and another bus ride from the babysitter's house to Felicity's house. Then Felicity had to walk up three flights of stairs to her apartment carrying her younger child, who was not yet walking. Claire had always asked Felicity to call Louisa Dyson first thing in the morning if she was ill and couldn't come to work, so that Mrs. Dyson could send a substitute. At eleven on July 19, Claire called Louisa Dyson. Mrs. Dyson tracked Felicity down and called Claire back to say that Felicity's son had diarrhea and she would be out for the rest of the week. Louisa Dyson, who was about to become Family Home Care's office manager, asked Grace D'Agostino, who would be the Quintons' new co-ordinator, to send Mrs. Quinton a substitute home attendant on the twentieth. Mrs. D'Agostino sent Eugenia Warren, a middle-aged woman who was also a far more accomplished home attendant than Felicity Sánchez. A few days earlier, Claire had learned that Medicaid would cover the cost of her mother's molded shoes. Eugenia Warren accompanied Kate and Claire Quinton to the shoe store by ambulette and stayed patiently with them for several hours while Mrs. Quinton waited her turn, while plaster strips were wrapped around her feet, and while they waited for the ambulette that would take them home. The Quintons were sorry to see Eugenia Warren go on the twenty-third.

On Monday, July 26, Claire had an errand to run. She went downstairs at five of ten and sat in the car waiting for Felicity. When Felicity hadn't come by ten-ten, Claire left to do her errand. When Claire returned, at ten-twenty, Felicity was standing on the sidewalk looking peeved that Claire hadn't been there to let her in. Claire told Felicity she was supposed to be there at ten. Felicity went upstairs. She was pleasant to Mrs. Quinton and told her she hadn't gone anywhere on her vacation.

At noon, Claire said, "Felicity, could you please tell me one thing. Why didn't you call me last Monday to say you weren't coming in?"

Felicity's answer was, "If you don't want me, Claire, I'll go."

When Claire said that wasn't the point, and asked her at what time she had realized she wasn't going to come to work and at what time she had planned to call, Felicity simply repeated, "If you don't want me, Claire, I'll go." That afternoon, Felicity started to leave shortly after five.

Claire told her she would have to stay until six. On Tuesday and Wednesday, Felicity said her husband had complained that she was getting home too late; until then, she had said he didn't get home until eight. The following day, Felicity said she didn't think she was going to work as a home attendant any longer. She told a few conflicting stories about her babysitting situation. On July 30, Felicity said she thought she would stay home and take in children while caring for her own. Claire telephoned Grace D'Agostino. She told Mrs. D'Agostino that she and her mother had been patient with Felicity but that enough was enough, and also that Yolanda Encalada, the current weekend home attendant, was no good. Claire said she needed someone who could take care of her mother — preferably someone reliable, to whom she could give a key, so that she wouldn't have to go downstairs every morning to let the home attendant in. Grace D'Agostino said that she could do nothing about Yolanda but that she would send the Quintons a new weekday home attendant starting August 9.

Saturday, August 7, was a dark day for Mrs. Quinton. Yolanda Encalada's humming and crude manners got on her nerves. "Wash yourself or you will smell like fish," Yolanda had told her that morning when she handed her a washcloth. Mrs. Quinton was worried about the new home attendant who would be coming on August 9. What if she proved to be another Mercedes Robbins? Although Mrs. Quinton had been told by the shoe store that her shoes would not be ready for at least six weeks, she exasperated Claire by asking her daily if anyone from the shoe store had called. On August 7, Mrs. Quinton said,

"Sitting in this wheelchair is the worst thing that has ever happened to me. No one was ever more active than I was when I was young." Mrs. Quinton had been in a similar predicament a year or so earlier, but in 1981 she had got rid of her wheelchair, and had even managed to walk downstairs. In August of 1982, she said she hoped that she would be able to walk downstairs by Christmas, but she had begun to fear that she would never be able to get downstairs on her own two feet again. After she told Dr. Romero how nervous Yolanda made her, he prescribed Valium for her. She still couldn't sleep. During the day, she would describe her sleepless night to Claire. As Mrs. Quinton lay awake in the early-morning hours of August 8, she couldn't bear to think of the future. Her thoughts turned to the past — all the way back to her childhood, when life had seemed as bright as a silver ribbon. She thought of her mother, a lighthearted woman who had sat up late sewing pinafores and chemises for her by hand. "Lord rest Ma," she said whenever she spoke her mother's name. She thought of her father, a quick-tempered but kind man ("Lord rest Dad") who was loved in the village where she was raised for nursing sick neighbors at night after he had come home from work, often staying with the sick until dawn.

<h2 style="text-align:center">◄§</h2>

Kate Quinton's mother, Delia Curran, was born in County Monaghan, Ireland, in 1873. She left school when she was thirteen and worked as a domestic at a local seminary. When she was eighteen, she emigrated to Glasgow, where wages were higher, and went to work as a maid for a Protestant minister and his wife. Kate Quinton's father, Robert O'Donoghue, was born in County Mayo, Ireland, in 1876 and attended school until he was eighteen. Before he emigrated to Scotland, two years later, he took his father's advice and changed his surname to Donoghue. His father had warned him of signs posted at places of employment in Scotland and England that read NINA — "No Irish Need Apply." Robert Donoghue was working as a surveyor's assistant in Glasgow when he spotted Delia Curran as she was leaving the minister's house to mail a letter. He contrived to meet her. While they were courting, he went to work as a laborer in a steel mill. They were married in April of 1901. Kate, their first child, was born ten months later. Their second child, Sheila, was born in 1903; their third, Anne, in 1904. In 1905, the steel mill sent Robert Donoghue to Newcastle upon Tyne, England, where the family lived for a year and a half in what Kate Quinton remembers as a "grand" house — one with a built-in bathtub. While the family was in England, Kate got scarlet fever. She spent four months in a hospital. During those months, her ears never stopped running. Half a century later, specialists in New York traced the loss of hearing in her right ear to scarlet fever. One of Mrs. Quinton's earliest memories is of feeling bored in the hospital. She looked out a window and saw some navvies working on a road. The men carried their lunches wrapped in red napkins. While the men's backs were turned, Kate sneaked out of the hospital, stole a red napkin, and ate the bread and cheese it contained. She told the nurses about her crime ("Open confession is good for the soul," she said recently) and was punished by being put under an ice-cold shower.

When the Donoghues returned to Scotland, in 1906, Robert Donoghue was given an opportunity to do contract work at the steel mill. He agreed to produce so-and-so much pig iron for so-and-so much money. He hired a few men to work for him, and, by prevailing upon them to work hard (and, when necessary, by working alongside them), he earned more than he had as a laborer. The Donoghues lived in Kirkintilloch, a town near Glasgow. They rented a fair-sized house with a large kitchen that had a coal fireplace. A metal tub was put in the kitchen on Saturday evenings for the children's weekly baths; the family shared a water closet out back with the people in the house next door. Robert Donoghue had been an outstanding student. Kate had inherited his scholastic aptitude. She started first grade when she was four and a half, and excelled at English (she still uses words elegantly, pronouncing them with a Scottish spin), geography (during many a night in the summer of 1982, as she lay in bed waiting for sleep to come, she recited the capitals of the countries of the world), history, and arithmetic. She has forgotten none of the bloody-minded behavior in the Ireland of Cromwell and "King Billy" (William III of Orange) and few of the lines of Robert Burns's poetry she was taught in Kirkintilloch's Catholic schools.

Kate Quinton recalls her childhood as carefree and agreeably filled with deviltry. At the age of three, she was attracted by the music of a Salvation Army band, and followed the sounds of tambourines and bugles for some distance; she was eventually dropped off at a police station. The police summoned her father and served her milk and cookies while they waited for him to fetch her. Christmases in the Donoghue household were festive. On Christmas Eve, each of the little girls hung one of the black hand-knit stockings they wore to school above the kitchen fireplace. When they came downstairs on Christmas morning, they found a lump of coal at the top of the stocking, a Valencia orange, an apple, and some small toys in the middle, and a poke of candy in the toe. There were also presents like dolls and rocking horses. Fruitcakes, currant cakes, fruit wines, and other special holiday food and drink were served on a lace tablecloth with fringes. In summer, the Donoghues took the overnight boat from Glasgow to Belfast and the train to County Monaghan. Delia Curran Donoghue crossed herself each time she reached Belfast, and said, "Thank God we're back in holy Ireland." Her husband's answer was "Not yet you're not. You're still in the North and it's full of unholy Protestants." The thatched-roof stone cottage of Delia Donoghue's mother was filled with pretty objects and offered many country pleasures — fresh milk from the creamery, butter to churn, fresh vegetables from the garden, and weekly rides in a pony trap to a nearby town for market day. Back home in Scotland, Robert Donoghue found time to show his children the latest wonders of the new century: the Lusitania, when it put in at Glasgow; some early airplanes flying in formation at Lanark.

As the family increased — Patricia was born in 1907, Eileen in 1909, Beatrice in 1913, and James in 1916 — the older girls had to drop out of school and go to work. Kate left school in the fall of 1916. She didn't care for her first job, in a canteen at the steel mill, and soon quit to go to work at Fitzgerald's, a grocery store within walking distance of her house. Mrs. Fitzgerald, the proprietor, was a widow who couldn't read or write. Her only daughter, a college graduate, had just found a job as a typist. For three years, Kate Donoghue boned, strung, and sliced hams, waited on customers, counted ration coupons, ordered groceries, and did the bookkeeping: her straight A's in arithmetic served her well as she added and subtracted in farthings, halfpence, sixpence, shillings, half crowns, guineas, and other eccentric coins of pre-metric Britain. In 1919, Mrs. Fitzgerald's daughter lost her job and took over Kate Donoghue's. Within two days, Kate had found a similar position at another store. She cherishes the reference Mrs. Fitzgerald gave her new employer: "capable, competent, and honest as the sun."

During the war, Scotland's steel mills had thrived on the demands of the armaments-makers. Work slackened soon after the Armistice. By 1919, Robert Donoghue was no longer a contractor; he was a laborer again. Many men were on the dole, and he foresaw harder times ahead. His brother Thomas had gone to Wilkes-Barre, Pennsylvania, some years earlier, and he sent him his passage. In 1920, Robert sailed for America, where his surname was further Anglicized to Donohue. He soon found a job in the coal mines of Wilkes-Barre. In 1921, he and two of his sisters sent passage for Kate and Sheila. They reached Wilkes-Barre on Halloween night; Kate remembers thinking that the natives of Pennsylvania wore very strange clothes. As a girl in Scotland, she had hoped to become a nurse. When she came to America, she thought it might be possible to study nursing, and was heartbroken when one of her aunts told her that she couldn't afford to do so.

~§

In 1921, a poor Irish girl in Wilkes-Barre had two choices — housework or factory work. Kate chose housework. Her first job — "the worst one I ever had" — was working as third maid for a couple named Hutchins who had three children. From 6:30 A.M. to 8:00 P.M., she made the beds, cleaned the bathrooms, and waited on table. She was paid thirty-five dollars a month, had Tuesday and every second Sunday off, and was not permitted to speak to her father when he telephoned her at work. She was homesick and didn't like living in other people's houses, but there was no turning back. After a few months at the Hutchinses', Kate's left foot hurt. When she was born, it was half a size smaller than her right foot. After her stay in the hospital with scarlet fever, her left ankle was weak. Special shoes with a brace for her left ankle were ordered at that time, but she was too vain to wear them. A doctor in Wilkes-Barre advised her to have an operation on the foot joint. She spent six weeks in a state hospital. The doctor who performed the operation operated on one of her left toes instead of on her left foot joint. The day she returned to the Hutchinses', she was told that her services were no longer needed. She soon found another job, as third maid for a wealthy couple named Finley. The pay was better (forty-five dollars a month);

she could count on getting time off for a rest in the afternoon; the Finleys' cook and waitress (two maiden ladies) were good company; the Finleys took her back in 1923 after she had to return to the state hospital to have her tonsils removed (a doctor yanked them out while she sat in a chair, and afterward she couldn't speak for several weeks); and she was the first third maid the Finleys had ever taken with them when they went to Lakeville, Connecticut, for the summer.

In 1923, Kate Donohue met Patrick Quinton, who had left his family's farm in County Mayo in 1920 to work in the coal mines of Wilkes-Barre, where some of his relatives had preceded him. He proposed to her shortly after they met, but she turned him down. She had made up her mind that she would never marry young or into poverty. In 1924, Patrick Quinton moved to Yonkers to work as a trolley-car motorman. Kate Quinton has kept some of the respectful letters he sent to her at the Finleys' from his boarding house in Yonkers, where he acquired a lifelong distaste for pot roast. Kate's sister Anne Donohue had immigrated to Wilkes-Barre in 1923. A year later, their mother left Scotland for Wilkes-Barre with the four youngest children. (Their passage was paid by Robert Donohue, Kate, Sheila, and Anne.) Delia Donohue sold most of her furniture and china; she thought it would be impractical to take them with her. She brought out only a few possessions — a blue-and-white English bone-china teapot that had belonged to her grandmother, a fluted silver rosewater dish she had bought at an auction, and a grandfather clock that had been a wedding gift. Kate, Sheila, and Anne helped their parents find and furnish a house in Wilkes-Barre before they left to seek their fortunes in New York.

Kate had never liked Wilkes-Barre: the climate was more extreme than Glasgow's, the city was ugly, the salaries were low, there was an excessive number of old maids. In 1925, after three years with the Finleys, it was time for a change. Mrs. Finley's married daughter helped her find a job as cook and housekeeper at eighty dollars a month with Honoria and Gregory Lawson, a couple in their late fifties who had recently moved from Philadelphia to a large apartment on New York's lower Fifth Avenue. Kate had never studied cooking, but she had a knack for it and copied recipes from cookbooks and women's magazines. One day while she was still in Wilkes-Barre, she decided to bake twelve loaves of bread. Her mother's bread, she couldn't help noticing, was leaden. Her bread was feathery light. All twelve loaves were gone in a matter of hours. "Now you see why I bake heavy bread," her mother said. "It lasts longer."

"The Lawsons were the nicest people I ever worked for, and that was the best job I ever had," Kate Quinton said not long ago. She liked being in complete charge of the household: she planned the menus; she chose the clothes that Mrs. Lawson wore when she went out in the evening; she oversaw the annual refurbishing of the apartment. Mr. Lawson, a prosperous businessman, was generous. He gave her seventy dollars a week for the table and never asked how she spent the money. Mrs. Lawson took Kate Donohue with her as her private maid when she visited friends in Raleigh, Washington, and Philadelphia, and made sure Kate always used the front door. Mrs. Lawson referred to her as "my little Kate," invited her out to lunch at Schrafft's, and borrowed money from her when she lost heavily at bridge.

When Kate Donohue went to work for the Lawsons, Mrs. Lawson asked her if she had a sister who could wait on table. Sheila Donohue had taken a course to become a manicurist, but her hands were not deft and she came to work for the Lawsons. Sheila got married a few weeks later, while the Lawsons were away for the Christmas holidays. Kate Donohue, who was her sister's maid of honor, held the reception at the Lawsons' apartment, with their silver and with some trepidation: they were out of town, and no one had told them about the wedding. In the spring of 1926, when Sheila admitted to Mrs. Lawson that she was married, and left, Anne Donohue replaced her and worked as the Lawsons' waitress for two and a half years. By then, Delia and Robert Donohue had moved to New York with the younger children. They lived in an apartment on Amsterdam Avenue at Ninety-ninth Street for several years. In the fall of 1929, they bought a house in the Windsor Terrace section of Brooklyn, because they wanted a house and preferred Brooklyn's trees to Manhattan's concrete. Robert Donohue worked for New York Edison when he first came to the city. He was laid off during the Depression, but Mr. Lawson got him a job as a painter at his office building and, later, as a maintenance man at the Lawsons' apartment building. Meanwhile, the other Donohue girls worked with Kate at the Lawsons' — Patricia for a year, Eileen for two years, and Beatrice, in 1931, for four months. Beatrice was the only girl in the family with a high school education, and she said to Kate, "Why should I have my diploma hanging above the kitchen stove when there's a job waiting for me at a life-insurance company?"

Soon after Kate Donohue moved to New York, she started going out with Patrick Quinton. They usually saw each other on her Thursdays and Sundays off. Sometimes they went out dancing (she bought shoes to fit her right foot and stuffed cotton into the toe of the left shoe) and sometimes they went to the Hippodrome. Once they went to hear John McCormack sing. Sometimes, if the Lawsons were away on Sunday, they would sit at the kitchen table with Kate's sisters and their beaus; on one occasion Patrick Quinton had to dash down the back stairs when the Lawsons returned earlier than expected. From time to time, Kate Donohue and Patrick Quinton quarreled, and Kate dated other young men. On December 31, 1930, he gave her an engagement ring. Shortly thereafter they had another falling out, but in October of 1931 they patched things up and told the Lawsons they were going to be married on November 15. They went together to Lambert Brothers, where Patrick Quinton bought his fiancée a platinum wedding band that he had inscribed "PQ to KD 11-15-31." Kate Quinton wore her engagement ring — a small diamond with two small sapphires on each side — and her wedding band until 1978, when her fingers became so thin that the rings slid off. The rings are now stored in their original boxes in a dresser drawer in her bedroom. Kate Quinton's wedding photograph is on the bedroom desk. She was a buxom bride of twenty-nine, who stood five feet five inches and weighed 126 pounds

— 20 pounds less than she had weighed six years earlier, when she was Sheila's maid of honor. Over the years, her auburn hair (which she has always considered her best feature) turned to champagne and then to pure white. As she grew older, she diminished in size; she is now five feet two inches tall.

The wedding was held in a church on Amsterdam Avenue near the apartment Kate's parents had first rented. The Lawsons attended the ceremony and gave the couple a hundred dollars in gold and a crystal frame for their wedding photograph. The newlyweds went by limousine to the Donohues' house in Brooklyn for the reception. When Mrs. Lawson's "little Kate" married, the Lawsons didn't lose a maid, they gained a butler. Driving a trolley car paid poorly, and, with jobs scarce in 1931, Patrick Quinton was glad to wait on table, do the heavy cleaning, and polish the silver for ninety dollars a month when the Lawsons asked him to work for them. The Quintons had comfortable living quarters at the Lawsons'. "We worked well as a team," Mrs. Quinton recalls. They stayed with the Lawsons even after a daughter, Barbara, was born, on October 3, 1934. Barbara lived with Sheila and her family; her parents saw her on their days off and every evening that the Lawsons didn't have company.

In 1935, Mrs. Lawson became seriously ill. For a while, she required nurses around the clock. Both Mrs. Lawson and Kate Quinton observed that Mr. Lawson spent a lot of time chatting with one nurse, a Miss Mercer. When Mrs. Lawson had to have a leg amputated, she seemed to know she was dying. She made Kate Quinton promise to select the dress she would be buried in, and made her promise to call her regular hairdresser and manicurist to do her hair and nails after her death. Kate Quinton was in the room with Honoria Lawson when she died, in March of 1936. She kept her promises. Shortly after Mrs. Lawson's death, Kate Quinton told Gregory Lawson that she was four months pregnant and that she was leaving. She and her husband had bought a complete set of furniture, had rented an apartment in Windsor Terrace near her parents, and were looking for a house to buy. "I can't bear to lose my whole little family at once," Mr. Lawson said, so she stayed with him until the end of July. Kate Quinton had treated her mother to a three-month trip to Ireland and Scotland that year. Her mother's ship back to America docked in New York on the morning of August 14. Kate and Patrick Quinton went to meet it. Kate Quinton felt labor pains at the pier but went to her mother's house in Brooklyn to listen to the latest news from Kirkintilloch. She called her obstetrician in Manhattan, who told her to go right to the hospital. Instead, she insisted on going to her apartment first to change her stockings, because one of the stockings she was wearing had a run. She left Brooklyn after 3 P.M. Claire Quinton was born at 6 P.M. In October, Mr. Lawson married Miss Mercer. She served skimpy meals. Patrick Quinton, who had continued to work for Mr. Lawson, quit a month later. He worked for modest wages at a florist's in Windsor Terrace for two years and then, at the outbreak of the Second World War, got a better job at an aircraft plant on Long Island.

In 1937, the Quintons found a house on Greenwood Avenue, two blocks from the Donohues'. The house cost

$3000. The Quintons spent another $5000 to convert it from a one-family house into a two-family house and to renovate it. They put in two new bathrooms, enclosed a porch, and had parquet floors laid. When Kate Quinton left the Lawsons', she was earning $105 a month, and she had saved most of her wages during her eleven years with them. The Quintons moved into the house in the spring of 1938 and stayed in it until the fall of 1946, when they moved a block north, to a house on Vanderbilt Street.

CHAPTER SIX

CLAIRE QUINTON HAS HAPPY MEMORIES of her childhood home on Greenwood Avenue and of the first two years the Quintons lived on Vanderbilt Street. Once she and Barbara were old enough to go to the parochial grade school in the neighborhood, they had many friends. Their classmates usually included at least one cousin. Kate Quinton's five sisters lived nearby with their husbands. Sheila had four children, Anne had seven, Patricia had five, Beatrice had three, Eileen had one. Patrick Quinton earned a decent living — in the early 1940s, his weekly paycheck was about $160 — and the tenants in the upstairs apartment on Greenwood Avenue paid $38 a month. Kate Quinton managed her own home as well as she had managed the Lawsons' home. She enjoyed being a wife and mother. Every weekday morning, she got up early, had a quick cup of coffee and a cigarette, got the girls off to school, and started on her housework.

Each day, she did some shopping, dusting, and sweeping; many days, before she prepared dinner, she baked a sheet or two of coconut kisses or a batch of brownies for Barbara and Claire and the friends they brought home. Certain days were devoted to certain tasks. She remembers her weekly routine of the 1940s with great pleasure.

On Sunday night, she soaked the clothes. On Monday morning, she washed the clothes on a washboard (she didn't get her first washing machine until the late 1950s), starched them (with homemade starch), and hung them up on a line to dry (she acquired her first dryer in the 1960s). On Tuesday morning, she ironed the clothes. In summer, she drank sarsaparilla while she ironed; Claire tried to hang around on Tuesday mornings, because she liked its root-beery taste. On Wednesday, Kate Quinton washed the sun-porch windows and polished them with a chamois cloth and got down on her hands and knees and waxed her floors with beeswax. On Thursday, starting in 1942, she went to her parents' house to do their heavy cleaning, because her mother had such bad arthritis in her knees that she could hardly walk. Robert Donohue had fallen a few years earlier and injured his shoulder. He could do only light work, and had become a night watchman. On Friday, Mrs. Quinton went to the fish market to buy oysters and fresh fish, and served oyster stew or fillet of whatever fish was in season (and often both oyster stew and fish) on Friday evening. On Friday night, the house was spotless. Kate Quinton believed that a workingman was entitled to enjoy the comforts of his home on the weekend and do nothing except a little painting, gardening, and puttering in the basement. Early on Saturday morning, Mrs. Quinton went to the super-market to do her major grocery shopping of the week. In midmorning, she went to the drugstore with Barbara and Claire to buy cod-liver oil, and to other small shops to buy whatever else she fancied. The girls loved the taste of cod-liver oil; Claire never had a cold until she was eighteen. On Saturday afternoon, Mrs. Quinton sham-pooed her daughters' blond hair and combed and twirled it around her fingers into corkscrew curls. When their curls needed trimming, she singed off the uneven ends with a match. Every second Saturday afternoon, she went to the beauty parlor and had a shampoo, a set, and a manicure for a dollar. One Saturday a month, she went to confession. Every Saturday, she baked apple pie, lemon-meringue pie, peach cobbler, pineapple upside-down cake, and/or sponge cake for Sunday. On Saturday night, be-fore she went to bed she polished the brass plate on the front door, so it would gleam for the Sunday churchgoers passing by.

Kate Quinton got up early on Sunday and went to six-thirty Mass. The Lawsons had eaten bountiful breakfasts, and Mrs. Quinton served a similar breakfast to her family on Sunday morning: orange juice or half a grapefruit; a large pan of corn bread; bacon and eggs with creamed potatoes, or corned-beef hash and fried potatoes. There was always company for Sunday midday dinner: usually Patrick Quinton's sister, her husband, and their two chil-dren, who lived in Queens; sometimes a couple of bache-lors Patrick Quinton worked with; and often a carful of Pennsylvanians. One Sunday, the menu was roast beef with browned potatoes, gravy, Yorkshire pudding, string beans, carrots, and salad with homemade French dressing. The next Sunday, it was roast loin of pork with gravy, homemade applesauce, candied yams, red cabbage, and salad. (To Kate Quinton, a meal with fewer than two vegetables was considered a snack.) Relatives almost always dropped by later in the day and ate leftover sliced roast meat, potato salad, and leftover cakes and pies. By 10 P.M., the last of the Sunday guests were gone, and it was time to soak the laundry.

On Monday evening, Kate Quinton went to the novena at her church. Every second week, she spent an evening playing bingo in the church auditorium. The highlight of her social life was the weekly meeting of her "sewing club." Eight women belonged to the sewing club, which met on Tuesday or Wednesday evening at eight. Every eighth week, when Kate Quinton was the hostess, she got up at six o'clock and started to prepare tomato aspics, orange molds with mandarin-orange slices, and the dainty tea sandwiches she had formerly served the Lawsons and their guests. She was proud that everyone looked forward to coming to Kate Quinton's because she served the best food, just as she was proud that her relatives congregated at her house on Sunday afternoons. No sewing was done at the sewing club, although someone usually asked someone else "How did your garment turn out?" and drew a laugh. The sewing club was a gossip club. On their weekly evening together, the women enjoyed eating, sipping highballs, and talking about clothes styles, the price of groceries, and their children. "We really had a lot of fun, but that's all in the past tense," Kate Quinton said recently.

In 1943, Kate Quinton became pregnant for the third

time; she gave birth to a sickly girl, who died a year later. In 1945, she began the change of life. She was hospitalized and, according to her doctor at that time, was close to a nervous breakdown. Patrick Quinton quit his job to care for his wife, his children, and his home, and took out a $2000 mortgage on the house on Greenwood Avenue. Kate Quinton was in bed for several months, and the Quintons had no health insurance. The doctor suggested that Mrs. Quinton was "charging along at a pace of a hundred miles an hour" and would be better off in a quieter place. The IND subway tracks ran under the ground adjacent to the Quintons' house. As the tracks became worn and the trains deteriorated, the house started to vibrate and its windows began to rattle. Kate and Patrick Quinton put their house on the market in the summer of 1946 and went, with Barbara and Claire, to a small town not far from Wilkes-Barre where Mrs. Quinton had relatives. Their plan was for Mr. Quinton to open a small business — perhaps a combination grocery store and gas station. After the Quintons had been in Pennsylvania for three weeks, Kate Quinton could take no more of the prescribed quietness. During their courtship, Patrick Quinton, who had inherited a large piece of land in Ireland, would joke that he wanted to return there to live; Kate always said she wouldn't be caught dead on a farm. Kate Quinton liked living at a pace of a hundred miles an hour. The Quintons returned to Brooklyn. A couple had made a thousand-dollar down payment on their house. The Quintons sold it for $10,000 and netted about $8000 after paying off the mortgage and the real-estate agent's fees and the closing costs. They bought a fourteen-room three-

family house a block north, on Vanderbilt Street, for
$12,500 with a $4000 mortgage. They moved into the first
floor of their house in November of 1946. Patrick Quinton
got a job working for a plastering company.

On Thursday, July 21, 1949, Patrick Quinton finished
a plastering job. On Friday, he went to a house in the
Bay Ridge section of Brooklyn to drop off materials for
a job that would begin on Monday. On Sunday, he didn't
feel well. Mrs. Quinton thought he had indigestion and
gave him a bottle of rhubarb and soda — a common
stomach remedy. Early on Monday, Patrick Quinton had
convulsions. Around ten o'clock, Kate Quinton telephoned
a doctor and a priest. The doctor took Patrick Quinton's
blood pressure — it was 248 over 130 — and told Mrs.
Quinton to call an ambulance. Shortly after Patrick Quinton reached the hospital, he lost consciousness. He died
before noon. High blood pressure ran in the Quinton family, but Patrick Quinton had always been a sturdy, healthy
man, and Kate Quinton was dazed by the suddenness of
his death. He was fifty-one when he died. She bought a
grave in a cemetery in Queens but visited it only twice,
within a few months of the burial. It took her two weeks
to recover from each visit. Kate Quinton plans to be
buried in the same plot as her husband. The grave has
no headstone. Mrs. Quinton is afraid of dying, and she
has asked Claire to take care of the headstone after her
death. The marriage had been a harmonious one, because
Patrick Quinton was an easygoing man and let his wife
do whatever she wanted. "As long as Kate's happy, I'm
happy," he often said. Patrick Quinton spoke softly, in a
light brogue, and was content to spend a Saturday after-

noon sitting in his blue lounge chair smoking a pipe and listening to classical music. He occasionally had a glass of beer or ale, but he never went to a saloon. Although Kate Quinton was widowed at the age of forty-seven, she never considered remarrying. "I never thought I'd find a man as fine as the one I had," she says. "My husband, Lord rest Pat, was such a good-living man."

❧

After her father's death, Claire Quinton began to realize that Barbara had always been her mother's favorite. Barbara took after her mother — she was prim and proper, she admired nice household furnishings, she was interested in cooking. Claire was a tomboy. She was happier with a hammer in her hand than with a spatula. When she returned home, her hair ribbons were untied and her clothes were stained. Her mother could tell whether she'd had a strawberry or a chocolate ice cream cone by the color of the splotch on her dress. Patrick Quinton never seemed to mind Claire's scuffed shoes or her fondness for sledding down Suicide Hill in a nearby park. "You enjoy your childhood so much," he had told her. She had been the first to greet him as he walked home from the subway after work. When she asked him to make her a slingshot or an orange-crate car on wheels, he had obliged her, despite his wife's obvious disapproval.

Patrick Quinton's paychecks were about two hundred dollars a week. After his death, Kate Quinton received Social Security survivors' benefits of sixty dollars a month for herself and her two daughters, until they reached the age of eighteen. There were always two tenants in the house, Patrick Quinton had left her a life-insurance policy, and Kate Quinton had some savings. Life went on. Her parents had sold their house when Delia Donohue could no longer take care of it, and had moved in with the Quintons a year and a half before Patrick Quinton's death. They brought with them the grandfather clock and the teapot that Delia Donohue had brought to America. The sewing club continued to meet. Kate Quinton's house was always filled with relatives on Sunday. When a daughter-in-law of one of her sisters died in childbirth, she took in the baby, who was retarded and blind, and kept him for eleven months; then the child had to be put in an institution.

In 1948, Barbara Quinton had started ninth grade at a well-regarded parochial high school for girls in downtown Brooklyn. Her tuition was ten dollars a month. In 1950, when Claire wanted to start ninth grade at the same school, her mother said she couldn't afford to send her. Mrs. Quinton insisted that Claire take the entrance examination for another parochial school that did not charge tuition. Claire didn't want to go there, and purposely failed the entrance examination. She told her mother she would put herself through the high school she wanted to attend. She took the test for Barbara's school and passed it. In ninth and tenth grades, she earned her tuition money by babysitting for one of her mother's tenants. As soon as she turned sixteen, she was able to get a job at Woolworth's. She worked there every afternoon after school and all day Saturday during her junior year and the first half of her senior year. During the last half of her senior year, she had an after-school job as a file clerk for a life-insurance company. Claire paid for her tuition and also for her books, her uniforms, her yearbook, and her class ring. Barbara did babysitting but was allowed to spend the money she earned on clothes.

Claire was popular in high school, and mischievous: she played hooky, she chewed gum, she whistled while she walked down the halls, which the nuns told her was something "ladies don't do." Claire was elected president of her class three times. Each time the principal was apprised of the election results, she insisted that a new election be held, so that someone who set a better example could hold the office. Claire was also popular with boys. In November, many of her classmates were praying to St. Jude, the patron saint of hopeless causes, for dates on New Year's Eve. Claire had a date by October. She graduated in June of 1954. Claire had wanted to be a nun ever since she was ten, but she agreed to work for a year or two before entering the convent. Barbara had met a young salesman named Dwight Gaylord in 1951; they were planning to be married in August of 1954. Claire paid for the dress she would be wearing as her sister's maid of honor. Her mother hadn't paid for her tuition, but Claire knew that her mother had been drawing savings out of the bank for several years, and that the Social Security payments would end on August 14 (Claire's eighteenth birthday), and she felt she owed it to her mother to help her replenish her savings. When she was Claire's age, Kate Quinton had given the money she earned at Fitzgerald's to *her* mother. Claire also knew she would have to spend several hundred dollars to buy the black oxfords, the black stockings, the undergarments, the white shirts, the habits, the winter and summer housecoats and nightgowns, and the toilet articles she would need for her first two and a half years in the convent — six months as a postulant and two years as a novice — before she took her first vows.

In June of 1954, Claire Quinton became secretary to a vice-president of an import-export firm in lower Manhattan. Her starting salary was fifty dollars a week; she gave twenty dollars a week to her mother. In September of 1954, Delia Donohue died in her sleep. The following month, Kate Quinton returned to work. She became a bookkeeper and receptionist for a cardiologist in Manhattan. She had liked keeping the books at Fitzgerald's, the money would come in handy (the house was old and needed new plumbing), and she enjoyed talking to the patients. Claire remembers being content at the import-export firm. She got along well with the other secretaries in the office and went out with them on coffee breaks; her work and her attendance were excellent (she received a five-dollar raise after a few months); she dated several young men. Everyone at the firm was surprised when she left, in February of 1956, to enter the convent.

Some of the novices at the novitiate on Long Island were surprised to see Claire when she came there and became a postulant: Sister Claire. They remembered her antics in high school. Sister Claire settled into a fairly rigorous life of prayer, meditation, college-level classes (in subjects ranging from art and music to religion), homework, and chores. In April, she got a bad cough. A doctor was called; he prescribed penicillin for her. She was taken to Brooklyn to have a chest X-ray (it was normal) and to speak to the Reverend Mother of the order. The Reverend Mother asked Claire how she thought she had got the cough. Claire said she didn't know. The Reverend Mother asked Claire if she wanted to go home. Claire said she didn't. When the Reverend Mother had interviewed Claire in 1955, she had given her a pre-entry warning: "No more shenanigans." Now she told her that when she said that, she hadn't intended for Claire to take life *too* seriously. She again suggested that Claire go home, and return if she got over the cough. Claire asked to stay on. The Reverend Mother agreed to let her live for six weeks at a different convent, in Brooklyn. Claire could sleep half an hour later, she could work with young children instead of going to classes, there would be less pressure.

By June, Claire's cough had improved, and she returned to the novitiate. In August, she became a novice and took the name Sister Mary Doreen. In March of 1957, she fell down a flight of marble stairs; she felt the effects of her fall three weeks later. At the beginning of April, she lifted a heavy piece of pottery in an art class; she felt a painful twinge in her back. A few days later, she walked into an English class. She started to sit down in a chair but her back locked: she couldn't sit down, she couldn't get up. She was assisted into bed. A doctor was called. He prescribed codeine. She was sent to another doctor, a psychiatrist. Between April and July, Claire was in grave pain. She could hardly tolerate the weight of the cincture and the rosary she wore around the waist of her habit. The psychiatrist who came to see her said, "Evidently, Claire, you have a problem, but it doesn't seem to be physical." In August, the Mistress of Novices met with Claire. She told her that her first year as a novice was almost over; she might be taking her first vows in one more year. Claire said she would like that, but she said she couldn't bend, and knew she couldn't last another year in the condition she was in. She said she realized she needed help for her back, which the order couldn't afford to give her. The Mistress of Novices and the Reverend Mother decided that Claire would leave the convent two days later. She accepted their decision philosophically. "You take your losses and your crosses," she says. One nun remained Claire's closest friend until her death, in 1981, and several other nuns are among her good friends today.

Before Claire entered the convent, she had given all her clothes to Barbara. When she returned home, her mother gave her the money to buy a new wardrobe. In September, Claire found a job as a secretary to the controller of a steamship company. That fall, she started going out with a young man named Peter Thorne, and she sought help for her back. Her mother's doctor gave her diathermy treatments; they didn't help. She went to a chiropractor; he snapped the bones in her neck and put pressure on different parts of her spine, but that didn't help, either. In the spring of 1958, Barbara's doctor sent her to a prominent orthopedic surgeon in Brooklyn, Dr. Joseph Morton. He gave her exercises to do, a lumbosacral corset to wear, and painkillers to take. In May of 1958, when the steamship company went bankrupt, Claire became an assistant to an executive at an investment-banking firm on Wall Street.

In 1958, the doctor Mrs. Quinton was working for was having personal and financial difficulties. She left her job. The only other job she could find was as a cleaning woman for a couple named Stern. Kate Quinton worked for the Sterns for the next thirteen years — usually three days a week. When she speaks of the Sterns, she speaks highly of them, but she prefers not to speak of them at all. It was a great disappointment to her to have to go back to working as a domestic. That year, she experienced a greater sadness. Shortly after Delia Donohue's death, Robert Donohue's eyesight failed rapidly. He could no longer read, and television bored him. He began to brood. He gradually became confused and unmanageable; he wouldn't bathe, he wouldn't eat properly. Then he became violent. He went after Kate Quinton with his cane. The third time he attacked her with his cane, she called an ambulance and had him committed to a psychiatric institution, where he remained until his death. As long as her father lived, Kate Quinton worried over what he thought about in his few lucid moments.

In 1959, Claire's back pains increased. She missed a few days of work during the summer. In September, she went to see Dr. Morton again. He examined her and told her to wear a spinal brace. A month later, she returned to him. The brace hadn't helped. Dr. Morton said Claire needed a spinal fusion. He told her she would have to spend about a month in the hospital after the fusion and at least six months at home resting, so that the fusion would solidify. Claire had plans to go to Europe with two friends the following May. She wanted to postpone the surgery. "Don't call me, I'll call you," she told Dr. Morton. She broke up with Peter Thorne; he took her to good restaurants and was a snappy dresser, but he was pushing her to marry him, and she wasn't in love with him. In March of 1960, Claire had to sleep in a beach chair for ten days — it was more comfortable than a bed — and missed two weeks of work. She canceled her plans to go to Europe. In May of 1960, she had her first spinal fusion. She was out on disability until March of 1961, when she returned to the investment-banking firm. Her back still ached, and pain radiated into her right leg.

In May of 1961, Claire met a young man named Jack Devlin. By 1962, she and Jack were dating steadily. Dr. Morton had prescribed muscle relaxants for Claire; they didn't work. She had to leave her job on Wall Street in August of 1963, because the trip from Brooklyn to lower Manhattan meant taking three subways, and the pain in her back was worse and had spread to her neck. She took a thirteen-day Caribbean cruise with three other young women and then went to work as a secretary to two certified public accountants in midtown Manhattan, where the salaries were higher and the opportunities seemed better. A neighbor gave her a ride to midtown each morning, and in the evening she could get home by taking a single subway. In March of 1964, Claire returned to Dr. Morton. He ordered some X-rays and said they looked fine, but in May of 1964 Claire had to leave her job because of the pain. She insisted that there must be something wrong, so Dr. Morton admitted her to the hospital and had a myelogram done. The myelogram — an X-ray of the spinal cord using a radio-opaque dye — showed a fissure: the fusion had never solidified. That month, Dr. Morton performed a second spinal fusion. Claire spent a good part of the next year flat on her back. Her back still hurt, so she returned to Dr. Morton in April of 1965. He sent her to a radiologist. She called Dr. Morton for the results of the X-rays. "Claire, you have a perfectly solid fusion," he said. She went to another doctor, who referred her to Dr. Kevin Twigg, a well-known orthopedic surgeon in Manhattan. In September, Dr. Twigg sent Claire to a radiologist. He told her that the fusion was not solid. Dr. Twigg performed a spinal fusion in October of 1965. Claire had fallen in love with Jack Devlin, who wanted to marry her. She broke up with him in October of 1966, because her back felt no better after three fusions than it had in 1957 when she left the convent. Kate Quinton was fond of Jack Devlin. If Claire married him, she said, she would sell her house and take an apartment not far from their home, and she would do all Claire's laundry, cleaning, and cooking. Claire was grateful to her mother, but she thought it would be unfair to Jack to marry him, because she believed that, with her back, she wouldn't be capable of having a child.

Claire was unable to work between May of 1964 and

July of 1967, and received disability payments from Social Security most of that time. One day in the winter of 1967, she felt particularly troubled, because her mother had to walk to the subway in the snow to get to the Sterns' while she stayed home. Claire resolved that she would make it up to her mother. That summer, she returned to work as an executive secretary at a brokerage house in lower Manhattan; she was still in pain, but she was able to drive to work and park on a pier near her office. In February of 1968, she treated her mother to a week-long Caribbean cruise. Kate Quinton, with her sisters Eileen and Sheila, set off for the Bahamas in style. She had a wardrobe of evening dresses, and gold and silver shoes to match them. Mrs. Quinton loved the luxury liner. "The breakfasts were like lunches, our beds were changed every day, they were turned down and our nightgowns were laid out every evening, and the tablecloths were changed after every meal," she recalls. In June of 1968, Claire took a leave of absence from her job. She had had constant pain in her right leg and her back since October of 1965. In June of 1968, Dr. Twigg performed another spinal fusion on her. It was a complete failure. In June of 1969, he performed still another spinal fusion, using a new technique. Claire's back felt better after the fifth fusion. She returned to work for the brokerage firm in March of 1970. In September of 1971, she was exhausted and asked the firm for a two-week vacation, to which she felt entitled after eighteen months of work. The firm refused to give her the vacation. She said she was going to take it anyway, and let them fire her, because by then she was planning to move out of the city. She went on a cruise and was careful not to get a suntan, because she was collecting unemployment insurance.

CHAPTER SEVEN

IN 1971, KATE QUINTON DEVELOPED diverticulosis, a
gastrointestinal ailment that afflicts many old people.
She suffered for thirteen weeks — her aging doctor did
nothing that alleviated her pains — but felt better four
days after she went to another doctor, who gave her a
chalky medicine to take. She put the Vanderbilt Street
house on the market in August. The house needed major
repairs; the property taxes had just gone up; the water
and sewer bills were rising. Kate Quinton could never
bring herself to raise the tenants' rents steeply. Another
reason the Quintons were thinking of moving out of Brooklyn was that Mayor John Lindsay had been threatening
to prohibit cars from entering Manhattan during the day.
Claire had been driving to work, because her back was
always better when she wasn't climbing up and down
subway stairs and being jostled on long subway rides.
The previous summer, the Lindsay administration had

curtailed sanitation services in Windsor Terrace — garbage was collected twice a week instead of three times a week — and increased them in poorer, denser sections, like Brownsville. The Quintons weren't sure the neighborhood would hold. Mrs. Quinton was sixty-nine, and she decided that the time had come to retire from her job at the Sterns'; she left them in October, after selling the house. She wanted to move to Teaneck, where Barbara and Dwight now lived, to be near Barbara and her grandchildren, Charles, Sarah, and Elizabeth. Her sewing club had stopped meeting many years before, her sisters Patricia and Beatrice and her brother James were dead, her many nieces and nephews had married and moved away: the full house on Sunday was also in the past tense. Claire thought that if she lived in Teaneck she would find a job she could drive to; parking in New Jersey would be neither a problem nor an expense. Barbara and Dwight Gaylord seemed pleased to have the Quintons move to Teaneck. They helped them find a house that was just a few blocks from their own house, and painted it for them. Kate Quinton had sold the house on Vanderbilt Street for $34,000. She cleared about $26,000 after paying off the mortgage, the real-estate commission, and the closing costs. The house in Teaneck cost $22,000. She assumed a $7000 mortgage. Mrs. Quinton had to buy a new refrigerator, and insisted on removing a wall oven in the house and replacing it with a new stove, because the wall oven wasn't big enough to hold her Thanksgiving turkey. She had about $8000 left by the time she had fixed up the house in Teaneck. The Quintons moved to Teaneck in May of 1972.

In June of 1972, Claire went to work as a secretary for a company in Wyckoff — an easy twenty-minute trip by car from Teaneck — for $145 a week. Her boss was very demanding, but she worked hard. Her salary was increased to $155 and then to $165. In May of 1973, she had chest pains and high blood pressure, but she went on working; her boss gave her four days off in July. In October of 1973, Claire and a friend went on a vacation to Nova Scotia. Claire returned with a bad cold but went back to work. After five weeks, she had almost no voice. She called to say she couldn't make it to the office. Claire's boss came to the house. He told her he was sorry, but he couldn't afford to have an employee out sick. He gave her a personal check for $200 and a company check for two weeks' pay. Claire's cold lasted until January of 1974. When she was able to go out job hunting, she couldn't find a decent job in New Jersey; everywhere she applied, she was told she was overqualified. In October of 1974, a cousin helped her get a job as a secretary and statistical typist at a ship-repair firm in lower Manhattan. She was out with the flu and low blood pressure in December of 1974 and January of 1975. The stress of the job and the two hours a day of commuting on the bus from Teaneck (plus the round-trip subway ride between the Port Authority Bus Terminal and lower Manhattan) were too much for her, and she quit at the end of May 1975.

Kate Quinton kept busy unpacking during her first two months in Teaneck. June 1972 was a dreary, rainy month, but the weather improved and she had a few visitors from Brooklyn over the summer. By September, she was edgy. She couldn't drive, there were no stores within walking distance — there weren't even any sidewalks on her block — and she could kill only one day a week polishing her silver. There wasn't much cleaning to do in a small house. Claire left for her job early in the morning and returned late in the evening. Claire had asked Barbara to take their mother to the supermarket once a week when she did her own grocery shopping. She warned Barbara not to go near her mother when she was buying a chicken: Kate Quinton tore open the see-through wrapping around the chicken with a fingernail, then smelled the chicken to see if it was fresh, and Barbara might be embarrassed. Otherwise, Claire assured Barbara, her mother's conduct in a supermarket was exemplary. Barbara took her mother to the supermarket three or four times; then she didn't telephone again to ask her to go shopping. Most of Kate Quinton's neighbors worked. She sat at home listening to the sounds of rustling leaves and cars whizzing by — sounds she loathed. She missed her friends and her three sisters still living in Brooklyn. Her friends called a few times, until they got their telephone bills. Teaneck was a long-distance call from New York City. In October of 1972, Claire asked her mother if she wanted to go to Brooklyn; she spent a happy week with Eileen, Sheila, and Anne, and had tea with Mrs. Stern. When she returned to Teaneck, she was looking forward to cooking her first Thanksgiving turkey for the family in her new oven. The Quintons spent Christmas at the Gaylords'.

In 1973, there were fewer visitors from Brooklyn, and Claire lost her job. In August of 1974, Kate Quinton was run-down. She was put in a hospital, for the first time in

almost thirty years, and spent a week there. In March of
1975, she fell and broke her elbow. The previous October,
there had been a slight to-do at the Gaylords' house. The
Quintons and one of their friends had been invited over
for a drink, and Claire had parked her car in its customary
place in the driveway. Dwight had to go out to buy some
milk. Claire's car was blocking his car. "Why the hell do
you always park your goddam car in my way?" he asked.
"Give me your car keys."

In May of 1975, four days after the Quintons had spent
a convivial Mother's Day with Barbara and Dwight at
their golf club, Barbara came over to visit her mother and
sister at eight o'clock in the evening.

As Claire recalls the conversation, Mrs. Quinton said,
"What a pleasant surprise, Barbara. How nice to see you."

"You sell this house, Mama, and get yourself an apartment in Brooklyn near one of your sisters," Barbara said.
"You, Claire, get yourself a pad in the city."

Nothing had prepared Claire for Barbara's outburst. She
didn't speak to her sister or brother-in-law from May until
August, when her mother, who hadn't been eating properly, lost her balance and fell again. Claire called Barbara
to ask her to take Mrs. Quinton to the hospital, because
her mother was so weak she didn't know what to do. Mrs.
Quinton was again in a very run-down condition. For two
years, she had been saying "You can't transplant an oak
tree." She had seen less of Barbara than she had expected.
Her grandson was away at college, and her granddaugh-
ters were busy with high school and junior high school
sports. She had started to suffer from arthritis; she blamed
it on Teaneck. Property taxes were going up, and so were

the prices of heating oil, gas, and electricity. The $8000 she had had when she came to Teaneck was gone. Claire had bought a 1970 Buick for $2750 in October of 1973, and she had missed work a good deal even before she gave up her last job, at the ship-repair firm, at the end of May 1975. Mrs. Quinton's monthly Social Security checks were small. Patrick Quinton had earned a decent salary for only a few years before his death, and Kate Quinton had chosen to collect Social Security widow's benefits at the age of sixty-two. "I might die when I'm sixty-three or sixty-four," she had said when Claire urged her to wait until she was sixty-five.

As soon as Kate Quinton got out of the hospital in August, she said, "Let's put the house up for sale and go back to Brooklyn." Claire was glad. The relationship with the Gaylords was a strain on her. She recalls that sometimes Barbara invited her to a cocktail party but said, "Mama can't come." Lindsay's car restrictions hadn't gone into effect; Claire thought it would be easier to get a good job in Manhattan than in New Jersey, and she would be able to drive to work. Rents were low in Windsor Terrace. The neighborhood had held. Claire gave a real-estate agent the exclusive right for sixty days to advertise and sell the house in Teaneck. Mrs. Quinton became impatient that the house wasn't sold immediately and, before the sixty days were up, gave another real-estate agent the exclusive right to advertise and sell it. Luckily, the first agent sold the house — for $34,000 — and there was no problem with the second agent. Claire had gone to the real-estate agent in Windsor Terrace who had sold the house on

Vanderbilt Street. He helped her find an apartment in a two-family house in Windsor Terrace for $200 a month. The apartment, at 283 Seeley Street, needed some fixing up. The Quintons had to pay $200 to the real-estate agent, pay a $200 security deposit, and pay $200 rent for the month of December while the apartment was being put in order. The place needed heavy cleaning, painting, carpeting in the foyer, $160 worth of new window shades, and a $400 refrigerator. (The refrigerator from Teaneck was a quarter of an inch too big to fit into the kitchen of the apartment.) By the time the Quintons moved into their apartment, on December 26, 1975, Kate Quinton had $23,000 left from the sale of the house in Teaneck.

The Quintons' new apartment was a few blocks from their former houses on Greenwood Avenue and Vanderbilt Street. The owner of the house lived in Delaware; his sister and her husband had the downstairs. Kate and Claire Quinton had a four-room apartment upstairs. In early 1976, Mrs. Quinton did all the unpacking. She could no longer go shopping, but she could get up and down the stairs to go to church, to get the newspaper, and to have tea with the owner's sister. Claire liked being back in Brooklyn; her close friend Helen Durbin had a house nearby. In May of 1976, Claire found a job at a plastics company in Manhattan. She was able to keep it for only three weeks, because of high blood pressure. (Claire Quinton sometimes suffers from high blood pressure and gets chest pains. At other times, her blood pressure is so low that she faints or blacks out.) At the urging of her local doctor, she went to the psychiatric outpatient clinic of a hospital in Brooklyn. Claire describes herself as a person who can face up to serious disappointments as they occur but who comes apart long afterward, when the reality of the disappointment sets in. She suddenly realized that her life hadn't turned out as she had expected it to, and felt as if she was a complete failure. She had had to leave the convent. She hadn't been able to marry Jack Devlin. (She had learned that he was happily married and had three children.) She had gone from being a young woman of eighteen who had perfect health and perfect attendance at her first job to being a woman of almost forty who had had five unsuccessful spinal fusions and who no longer kept jobs. Her back had started to hurt a great deal during her last year in Teaneck. The dry cough she had first got in the convent kept recurring. Hardly a year went by that she didn't have a bad cold or a case of flu for two months of the winter. She periodically felt overwhelmed by her mother's demands. She had fled the house in Teaneck in February of 1974 to spend two days with a friend. She had left 283 Seeley Street in June of 1976 to stay with another friend shortly before seeking psychiatric help.

In January of 1977, Claire fell down on a driveway near 283 Seeley Street and broke her right leg and ankle. She spent three weeks in the hospital. The bones didn't mend well. Her leg was in a cast for five months. She filed for disability in September of 1977, because of her back and her leg, and didn't get it. Kate and Claire Quinton liked their apartment at 283 Seeley Street and were sorry when the owner told them, in the fall of 1977, that he wanted to move his own family back into it. They found a four-

room, ground-floor apartment a block and a half away, for
$250 a month, and moved in on February 1, 1978. The
front door was at street level, and a door in Claire's bedroom opened onto a shady back yard. Mrs. Quinton's
arthritis had been bothering her. Claire thought a ground-
floor apartment would be sensible. Her mother didn't care
for the apartment. She complained that water bugs were
running rampant. She didn't like the pine tree in the front
yard, which made the living room dark. She didn't like
the looks of a gray house across the street. She didn't want
to sit in the back yard.

In April of 1978, Claire became severely depressed. She
telephoned her therapist, who urged her to go to the hospital with which her psychiatric clinic was affiliated. Her
mother opposed her going. The therapist told Claire to put
her mother on the telephone and asked Mrs. Quinton to
give Claire the money to get to the hospital by car service.
Claire underwent many tests during her hospital stay. The
psychiatrists diagnosed her as suffering from neurotic depression. She spent the eight days in the hospital in a
wheelchair, because her back and her leg hurt so much.
In July of 1978, she went back to Dr. Twigg, who sent her
to a radiologist. The X-rays looked all right to Dr. Twigg,
but Claire was still in pain, so he had her admitted to the
hospital, where a myelogram was done. He called in a
neurosurgeon for a consultation. The neurosurgeon was in
favor of operating. Dr. Twigg said the myelogram showed
that the last fusion was solid. "You don't need an operation, but you do look very washed out," he told Claire.
"Stay in the hospital an extra few days." In October of

1978, Claire had another disability hearing. The judge seemed to be impressed by the psychiatric testimony, and granted her disability. It was retroactive for one year, and she got a check from Social Security for $6000. Kate Quinton insisted on moving out of the ground-floor apartment as soon as their one-year lease was up. Claire went back to the real-estate agent. He told her that there was an apartment available at 292 Seeley Street, almost directly across from 283 Seeley. Kate and Claire Quinton had liked the block, with its well-maintained brick houses. Claire went to see the apartment with Helen Durbin one evening, after Helen got home from work. The apartment was cold, but the landlord said he would heat it properly. It was in good shape. The rent was $265 a month. The Quintons moved in on February 1, 1979. Mrs. Quinton was soon dissatisfied with the apartment. The landlord didn't live up to his commitment to heat the house. His wife used a lot of garlic in her cooking. Garlic was one of Mrs. Quinton's least favorite aromas. In February of 1980, he raised the rent to $300. In the fall of 1981, after the rent was increased another $45, Barbara bought her mother an electric heater.

Kate Quinton also associated the new apartment with a precipitous decline in her health. In the spring of 1980, she had violent stomach pains. In June of 1980, she spent three weeks in a hospital in Brooklyn. Her ailment was diagnosed as diverticulosis, and she was put on a bland diet. After she got home, she still had pains. She went to Barbara's house in July. Barbara put her in a hospital in New Jersey in August. Once again, she had diverticulosis and was put on a bland diet. Barbara was angry with her for not complaining enough: the hospital discharged her after eight days. In 1979, Kate Quinton's sister Sheila had put her house in Brooklyn up for sale. She was planning to move into a housing complex for senior citizens in Connecticut to be near several of her children. She sold the house much sooner than she had expected, and rented a basement apartment next door to the Quintons', on Seeley Street, from the fall of 1979 until the fall of 1980, when her apartment in Connecticut became available. One Sunday evening in September of 1980, Kate Quinton went down to have dinner with Sheila. After dinner, her legs buckled. She couldn't walk up the stairs. Sheila brought her a chair. Some neighbors carried her up to bed. The arthritis in her knees was becoming more debilitating. She had stomach pains and no appetite again. Janet Grafton, a family friend who was a visiting nurse, gave Kate Quinton a walker and a commode. In the winter of 1980, Claire Quinton rented a wheelchair with a built-in commode for her mother. By February of 1981, Kate Quinton was confined to her wheelchair and her bed. Barbara wasn't satisfied with the Brooklyn doctor who had treated her mother for diverticulosis in 1980. In March of 1981, she found another doctor for her, through a friend of a friend — Dr. William Ruffolo, who was affiliated with Lutheran Medical Center, where he had done a residency in family practice. Dr. Ruffolo came to the Quintons' apartment three times in March. He treated Kate Quinton for her arthritic pain and her abdominal pain. On one of these visits, Dr. Ruffolo recalled later, Claire told him that her mother had drunk a bottle of gin and a bottle of something else (he didn't remember what) the previous evening. He had never seen any evidence of drinking in the Quinton household himself. He continued to talk to others as if he believed what Claire had said, however, and said that he thought Claire, too, had a penchant for drinking.

Janet Grafton had told Claire about Nursing Sisters Home Visiting Service, a certified home health agency that provides short-term help to people who are ill, and advised her to ask Dr. Ruffolo to refer her to it, which he did in early April of 1981. On April 10, a nurse from the agency's Park Slope office, which served Windsor Terrace, came to see the Quintons. She decided that Mrs. Quinton needed a physical therapist to get her out of her bed and wheelchair and back onto the walker; a nurse to care for a rash she had developed on her buttocks and to encourage her to improve her eating habits; and a home health aide. The nurse also decided that a medical social worker was needed to help Claire cope with her willful mother.

Evan Flint, a physical therapist, started to come to the Quintons' in late April. Kate Quinton seemed to have adapted to the role of invalid. She resisted doing the exercises she was supposed to do. She wouldn't move a small table in her hall, which got in the way of the walker and the wheelchair. The nurses who visited periodically in April and May found Mrs. Quinton "self-directed" — their way of saying that she did pretty much as she pleased. She ate as little as she wanted, smoked as much as she wanted, and once refused to let a nurse examine her raw buttocks. Dr. Ruffolo came to examine them in May. The

medical social worker, whose name was Florence Franklyn, first visited Mrs. Quinton in late April. She found her
depressed and full of complaints. Mrs. Quinton often
seemed to complain for the sake of complaining. She said
the apartment was cold and the landlord crude and rude,
but she showed no interest in moving when that was proposed to her. Kate Quinton conveyed the impression that
her problems weren't just physical ones but the emotional
problems of old age as well. She had outlived many of her
friends and relatives, and felt lonely and useless. Her sister
Anne had recently died. She told Miss Franklyn she missed
seeing Sheila now that Sheila had moved to Connecticut.
She saw little of Eileen, who lived in Flatbush, because
Eileen spent every day playing bingo. Mrs. Quinton took
a dark view of ever regaining her health. She considered
selling the house on Vanderbilt Street a "major mistake,"
because there she had had "more independence and more
control." Florence Franklyn got in touch with Selfhelp, a
local service center for senior citizens, to get Kate Quinton
a home-care worker, because Nursing Sisters Home Visiting Service couldn't provide one on a long-term basis. Mrs.
Quinton told Florence Franklyn that she had ten thousand
dollars in the bank. She wouldn't spend any money on a
home attendant or on a pair of molded shoes that Evan
Flint said she needed to help her walk. Miss Franklyn told
Selfhelp that Kate Quinton had only five thousand dollars.
She knew that that was close to the maximum amount a
person could have and still get free home-care service from
Selfhelp. She was willing to halve Mrs. Quinton's assets
not for her sake but for Claire's. "The burden wasn't fall-

ing on Kate Quinton, it was falling on Claire," Florence Franklyn says. She noticed that Mrs. Quinton spoke more pleasantly to other people than she did to Claire, that she found fault with Claire's cooking, and that Barbara was obviously her favorite daughter. Her eyes sparkled when she spoke of Barbara.

In early May, Mrs. Quinton became slightly more co-operative — the table in the hall was finally moved into Claire's room — but she refused to elevate her swollen feet and declined large-type books. The situation in the Quinton household reached a crisis in mid-May, after Claire injured her back while trying to lift her mother. Mrs. Quinton felt a combination of guilt that Claire had hurt her back and anger that because Claire had hurt her back she couldn't do as much to help her. She made it clear to Florence Franklyn that Claire could never meet the high standards she had set for herself and had been able to live up to. She had never failed her own mother, she said. Mrs. Quinton let Claire know this, and as result Claire felt angry and trapped. Florence Franklyn believed Mrs. Quinton needed more than four hours of home care a week — the maximum Selfhelp provided any client. She was more of a burden than Miss Franklyn felt that Claire could bear. Claire could scarcely leave the apartment to shop. When Miss Franklyn told Kate Quinton she needed more home-care hours and would have to pay for them, she said she couldn't afford to pay, and started to cry. She said she preferred to rely solely on Claire. When Claire told Florence Franklyn that Barbara had once offered to pay for a distant relative to help out with her mother if things got very bad, Mrs. Quinton reluctantly consented to accept Barbara's offer of help. Claire said she would call Barbara. After eleven days had gone by and Claire hadn't called Barbara, Florence Franklyn called her. Barbara said the relative she had previously offered was no longer available. When Miss Franklyn proposed hiring a home attendant privately for about eight additional hours a week, at a cost of about twenty-five dollars a week, Barbara said she couldn't afford it. Florence Franklyn's impression was that Barbara sounded defensive. She said that she had children in school and that her mother was stubborn. It seemed to Florence Franklyn that Barbara was not the wonderful doting daughter Mrs. Quinton had wanted her to believe Barbara was. Barbara said she would call Miss Franklyn back if she could help pay for the home attendant. She never called. Florence Franklyn believed that Barbara could have afforded the money if she had wanted to spend it.

In late May of 1981, just as Mrs. Quinton was getting over a bad rash on her buttocks and was walking twenty or thirty feet a day with the walker, a nurse discovered a lump in her right breast. Dr. Ruffolo was on vacation. He came to see Mrs. Quinton immediately after he returned, on June 3. He said he would admit Mrs. Quinton to Lutheran Medical Center as soon as a bed was available. He couldn't get a bed, so he admitted her to Lutheran by way of the emergency room on June 9. The lump was removed; it was benign, and Kate Quinton returned home on June 28.

The home-care worker from Selfhelp resumed her visits

in July, and Evan Flint returned that month to give Kate Quinton physical therapy. Mrs. Quinton's outlook was brighter than it had been before the breast operation, and she and Claire seemed to be getting along better. Prior to the operation, the director of the Nursing Sisters' Park Slope office had decided that the Quintons no longer needed a medical social worker. Shortly after her return home, Kate Quinton told Claire to return the rented wheelchair, and started to use the walker. By the end of August, Evan Flint had her walking up and down the stairs; his mission accomplished, his visits stopped. In late August, Kate Quinton went to Teaneck to see Barbara and Dwight there for the first time since the previous Christmas.

In September, Mrs. Quinton's condition started to decline. Once again, her buttocks were raw. Dr. Ruffolo made one house call, and a dermatologist, to whom he had referred Mrs. Quinton, made two house calls. Mrs. Quinton gradually became weaker. She used the walker, but she couldn't get up and down the stairs. Claire had made plans to go to Lake Winnipesaukee with Helen Durbin in the fall. She got a bad case of the flu and had to cancel her travel plans. In mid-October, she was so discouraged about her own health and her mother's deterioration that she telephoned Selfhelp to inquire about nursing-home placement for her mother. Barbara and Dwight came in for Thanksgiving dinner and, in mid-December, for an early Christmas dinner. They were going to fly to Arkansas to spend the holidays with their son, Charles, and his family.

Although Mrs. Quinton was far from well at Christmastime, neither she nor Claire had any idea that on January 5, 1982, she would be in such pain that she would be admitted to Lutheran Medical Center, would stay there for almost two months, come close to being sent to a nursing home, return home instead on T.C.P. in March, and make the acquaintance of fifteen home attendants over the next five months.

CHAPTER EIGHT

WHEN LOUISA DYSON WAS PROMOTED to office manager at Family Home Care Services, Grace D'Agostino became Kate Quinton's case coordinator. Mrs. D'Agostino looked at the long list of home attendants that Mrs. Quinton had had since early March and thought she must be a problem client. Louisa Dyson assured her that this wasn't true — that Mrs. Quinton had simply been an unlucky client as far as home attendants were concerned. Mrs. D'Agostino knew of an excellent home attendant who was looking for a nine-to-five job. She telephoned Claire and asked if those hours were acceptable. Kate Quinton was getting up earlier than she had when she went home on T.C.P., and Claire said they were. The woman was Jasmine Pagano, who owned a two-family house near Grace D'Agostino in Bensonhurst. Jasmine Pagano had become a home attendant in April of 1982. She had been assigned to work eight hours a day, seven days a week, for two women who shared an apartment — a ninety-year-old retarded woman and an eighty-one-year-old blind woman, who often attacked her retarded housemate. As the condition of both women declined, the case became a twenty-four-hour case, though Jasmine was paid for only twelve hours of work. She stayed on, sleeping in a room with the blind woman, because she felt a human commitment to the women, and also because she wanted the extra four hours' wages; her husband, Emilio, had been laid off in the spring from his job as a roofer and was collecting unemployment insurance. Jasmine's younger son, Victor, who was five, complained that he wasn't seeing his mother enough. She gave her oldest daughter, Donna, the job on weekends, but five days a week away from her family were still too many. In August, she requested a five-day-a-week, eight-hour-a-day job.

Jasmine Pagano, a sturdily built, animated Trinidadian woman in her late thirties, came to the Quintons' on August 9. The first words she said, in a disapproving tone, were "Oh, this kitchen floor. It should have a shine." Claire explained her mother's daily routine and showed Jasmine where everything was. Jasmine caught on quickly, had strong arms, and handled Mrs. Quinton easily. After Mrs. Quinton had had her breakfast, Jasmine said, "All right, Kate, you have to go bye-bye" and had Mrs. Quinton wheel herself into the living room, where she could look out the window to see what was happening on Seeley Street. "I always do the kitchen and bathroom floors every day," Jasmine said, and she took both rooms by storm. She scoured the bathtub, she polished the kitchen cabinets. Then she dusted and vacuumed Mrs. Quinton's bedroom and did all her personal laundry. After the cleaning and washing were done, she made an eggnog for Mrs. Quinton and sat down to chat with her while she ate her own lunch — a sandwich she had brought from home: mayonnaise was spread on one piece of white bread, grape jelly on the other, with some American cheese in the middle; the grape jelly had soaked through the bread. (Claire eventually prevailed upon Jasmine to use the Quintons' strawberry preserves.) After lunch, Jasmine got Kate Quinton to use the walker, supervised her exercises, massaged her legs, and helped her prepare dinner.

Before Kate Quinton went into the hospital, she had watched *Another World* on TV at two o'clock every day. She had lost track of the soap opera's characters while she was at Lutheran and had shown no interest in watching it for months after she got home. Claire thought that *Another World* broke up the day for her mother, so she encouraged her to watch it. Watching it with Jasmine was fun. Jasmine took the characters very seriously, offering a running commentary on their misdeeds and clapping when the plot became particularly exciting. In the fall, Kate Quinton and Jasmine Pagano added a 3 P.M. show called *Fantasy* to their television-viewing schedule. At four o'clock, Jasmine said, "It's Snowy Bleach time, Kate," and they went into the kitchen. Kate Quinton's dentures were more than twenty years old and had become stained from use and from smoking. Baking soda no longer made them bright enough, so she brushed them with and rinsed them in bleach. Then she and Jasmine finished preparing dinner. Before Jasmine left, she carried Claire's small black-and-white TV set from Claire's room into the kitchen, so that Mrs. Quinton could watch the news at five o'clock. One day during Jasmine's first week at work, Claire heard the grandfather clock in the hall strike the hour of five. She told Jasmine that it was time for her to go home. "No, I want to hear the end of Kate's story," she said. Kate Quinton told Jasmine a few stories about her past — about the day she had learned to swim in Lakeville, Connecticut, by simply plunging into the water and nearly drowning — and was delighted to have such an appreciative audience.

Mrs. Quinton was somewhat guarded about her past — she never let on that she had been a maid — and preferred to listen to Jasmine's confidences. Jasmine had married as a teenager in Trinidad and had two daughters with her first husband. While he was away working on another part of the island, he heard rumors that Jasmine was being unfaithful to him. He divorced her before discovering that the rumors were false. Jasmine came to the United States in 1967 to live with an aunt in Brooklyn. She soon found work in a factory. She met Emilio Pagano there, and they married several years later. Jasmine eventually sent for her daughter Donna, who is now nineteen. Her second daughter still lives with her father in Trinidad. Jasmine and Emilio, a Costa Rican, had three children — Raymond, twelve, Dora, eleven, and Victor. They bought their house in 1974. To Kate Quinton, Jasmine's life had soap-operatic possibilities. One day, Jasmine told her that Donna had accepted some long-distance collect calls from a boyfriend in Trinidad; Jasmine's telephone bill was $180. She couldn't pay the bill, and the telephone was disconnected. If the Quintons wanted to reach her, they had to call the couple who rented her second floor. One day, Emilio — who often got drunk — threatened to beat Donna; she moved out and lived with one of Jasmine's relatives for a few weeks. One night when Emilio got drunk, he was banished from Jasmine's bed for a while. Another night when he was drunk, he fell down a flight of stairs. One day at school, Victor was given an ear test. He was told to raise his hand whenever he heard something. When the school informed Jasmine that Victor had a hearing problem, Victor admitted that he hadn't felt like raising his hand. "I must have that child baptized to get the demons out of him," Jasmine told Mrs. Quinton.

Cindy Strong, the T.C.P. public-health nurse who had outlined the tasks that home attendants were expected to perform in the Quinton household, had written on Kate Quinton's T.C.P. chart that one of the home attendant's tasks was to "encourage daughter to take naps or rest and go outside to provide some relief from constant care of patient." Jasmine understood this aspect of her job. She arrived punctually every morning and kept Kate Quinton happily occupied, so that Claire was able to get out when she felt well and had things to do, and was able to stay in her room when her back ached. In the evening, after Jasmine left, Claire heated the dinner and ate with her mother. Claire felt that "at five o'clock, when I come on duty, I'm a fresh face," and her mother had something to talk about — all the things Jasmine had told her. Jasmine and Claire did each other favors. When Jasmine was broke, she borrowed money from Claire. When Claire embroidered a growth chart for Charles's son's birthday that required finishing on a sewing machine, Jasmine asked her tenant to do it on her machine. As Claire's weight continued to decline — by November she weighed 150 pounds and was wearing size 14 pants — she gave Jasmine many of the clothes that were now too big for her. When Claire was sick, Jasmine cleaned Claire's room, which wasn't in her job description, and she tried to encourage Claire. Whenever Mrs. Quinton praised Barbara, Jasmine reminded her it was Claire who had kept her out of a nursing home. In September, Kate Quinton called Grace D'Agostino to tell her she could no longer tolerate Yolanda Encalada on weekends. Mrs. D'Agostino replaced her with Suzanne Blanc, a shy young Haitian who had few skills and a sickly nature; she often sat with her head in her hands or spent hours in the bathroom. Mrs. Quinton dreaded the weekends with Suzanne but got through them by thinking that on Monday morning at nine she would see Jasmine's bright smile.

Jasmine Pagano was a great comfort to the Quintons in the fall and winter of 1982. The shoe store had finally called, and on September 7 Jasmine set off by ambulette with Kate and Claire Quinton to fetch the molded shoes. Kate Quinton telephoned Evan Flint on September 8. She didn't hear from him right away. Claire had forgotten that a doctor would have to call Nursing Sisters Home Visiting Service before a nurse would come to the house to make an assessment and reinstate service. Evan Flint gave Mrs. Quinton physical therapy eight times between October 15 and November 12. Even with the molded shoes, Kate Quinton could do little walking. Evan Flint's main goal was to assist her in walking up and down the stairs. She could only get down and up three steps. Evan Flint observed that she was unable to walk up without great pain.

Mrs. Quinton's hopes of walking downstairs by Christmas were gone.

As soon as Kate Quinton had her molded shoes, she started to nag Claire about her eyeglasses. Claire made a number of calls before she found an optometrist who would take Medicaid, and then she arranged for free transportation to his office by ambulette — another time-consuming procedure that she had mastered for the trips to the shoe store in July and September. The optometrist who tested Mrs. Quinton's eyes on October 11 determined the strength of the lenses she needed and let her select new frames. He was grumpy, but his assistant was kindly and offered to drop the eyeglasses off at her home, and did, on October 21. With the new glasses, Kate Quinton's eyes stopped tearing, and she could see a little better. As soon as she had the glasses, she told Claire to make inquiries about new dentures, for which Medicaid would also pay. Hers were worn and had become too big for her over the years; she could no longer chew meat. She also asked Claire to buy two electric radiators. The apartment was still frigid except for the area immediately next to the electric heater Barbara had bought. Claire went to Macy's to buy the new radiators, but Mrs. Quinton fell sick again before Claire could get around to finding a dentist who would accept Medicaid.

Starting in July 1982, Mrs. Quinton had seen a doctor from Family Physician Service periodically. Dr. Louis Romero had come to the house when she had had an ear infection in mid-July. One of his colleagues had come on August 1, when she had had a urinary-tract infection. Dr. Romero had visited her twice in August and once in September. He had told her that he wanted to get to know her and would visit her every second Thursday. He had returned to the house only once, in early October, when she telephoned him to say that her bones ached, that she was nauseated, and that she had the flu; he had prescribed the appropriate medications.

On the evening of October 29, Claire's friend Veronica O'Connell came in from Long Island for three days. Claire had a good time going out with her. On Saturday, they saw *E.T.* and drove around Greenwood Cemetery admiring the elaborate monuments. On Sunday, they went to church, saw *An Officer and a Gentleman*, ate pastrami sandwiches in a luncheonette, and did some shopping. When they returned, they had a good dinner with Mrs. Quinton, who had done the cooking. After dinner, Kate Quinton said she was feeling tired and went to bed. At 10:05 P.M., Veronica was taking a shower and Claire was watching *Trapper John M.D.* She heard her mother cry out, "Claire, Claire, I can't breathe!" Claire called Family Physician Service and then an ambulance. She and Veronica accompanied Kate Quinton to Lutheran's emergency room, where one of Dr. Romero's colleagues took a chest X-ray, and told her to stop smoking at once. He said he didn't like to admit elderly patients to the hospital unless it was absolutely necessary, and sent her home by ambulance at 1:50 A.M.

On Thursday, November 11, Kate Quinton felt ill. She didn't eat anything. She became disoriented: at 10:20 P.M. she woke up and asked Claire where Jasmine was. She didn't eat on Friday. On Saturday, she became incontinent. On Sunday morning, she decided to get herself out of bed and into the wheelchair; she fell out of the wheelchair. Claire strained her back picking her up and helping her back to bed. That evening, Kate Quinton was again disoriented. On Monday, November 15, her pains increased. In the afternoon, Claire telephoned Family Physician Service. In the early evening, one of Dr. Romero's colleagues came to the house, examined Mrs. Quinton, and decided to admit her to the hospital. She had a urinary-tract infection and was dehydrated. The infection cleared up with antibiotics, and she was soon rehydrated on I.V.s. She was occasionally disoriented. "Please get out of my kitchen," she told a nurse. One afternoon, she said to Jasmine, who visited her faithfully, "It's five o'clock. Time to go home. I'll see you tomorrow morning at nine." Mrs. Quinton didn't want to eat lunch in her room; the nurses humored her by letting her eat at the nurses' station. She became irascible when anyone mentioned the word "hospital," and protested when Claire tried to order her a television set; she didn't want a television set — she wanted to go home. She asked the nurses where Claire was before visiting hours and was nasty to Claire when she came to the hospital shortly after visiting hours began. On November 21, she accused Claire of having an orgy in her bedroom "with fifty men." Claire walked out of her mother's room. Kate Quinton was sent home on Monday morning, November 22.

Back in July, Barbara Gaylord had invited her mother out to Teaneck for a visit. At Claire's insistence, Mrs. Quinton hadn't simply declined the invitation but had given her reasons for declining it. She had told Barbara she was hurt that Barbara had wanted to put her in a nursing home. "The day you make any plans for me, I'll be six feet underground," she said. In late August, Barbara had called her mother to say that she and Dwight were going to be in Brooklyn for a wedding and wanted to stop by. This time, Claire had prevailed upon her mother to tell Barbara how angry she had been when Dwight had telephoned Claire the previous February to say that his mother-in-law was a senile bitch who belonged in a nursing home. Barbara had replied that Dwight didn't say she was senile. "All Dwight said was that you could be a bitch, meaning that you could be stubborn," Barbara had said. Mrs. Quinton had told Barbara she was welcome to visit her but Dwight was not. Barbara had said she wouldn't come alone.

At the beginning of October, Claire received a letter from Barbara:

> Dear Claire,
> I am sorry for what has happened.
> I had no right to talk to you in that way.
> I hope you will accept my apologies. I went to say I'm sorry at Sarah's wedding but you turned away. I hope you don't turn away now.
> Love,
> Barbara

Kate Quinton cried when Claire showed her Barbara's note; she was eager for a reconciliation. Claire was not. She didn't call Barbara for more than two weeks. She told Helen Durbin she knew that Barbara had written her partly because she felt guilty and partly because the holidays were coming. A week later, Claire spoke to Barbara on the telephone. "After all, we are sisters and the holidays are coming," Barbara said. Claire told Barbara that she accepted her apology and didn't mind talking to her on the telephone but that she didn't want to go to Teaneck before she got a few things cleared up. She said she was sick of feeling that Barbara and Dwight only tolerated her and her mother, as they had when the Quintons lived in Teaneck and as they had the weekend of Sarah's wedding. "Oh, no, that's not the case," Barbara said. "Can you think it over and I'll call you back?"

Claire told her mother to go to Teaneck for Thanksgiving alone; she would spend the holiday with friends. Kate Quinton said she wouldn't go to Teaneck without Claire. The next time Helen Durbin talked to Claire, Helen asked her, "How many more years does your mother have left? It would mean so much to her." In early November, Claire agreed to go to Teaneck for Thanksgiving. "I usually don't buck my mother," she told another friend. "I'm like my father. I give in." In mid-November, Claire's psychiatrist increased her anti-depression medication, because of her anxiety about going to Teaneck. After Kate Quinton went into the hospital on November 15, Claire hoped that the Thanksgiving trip to Teaneck would be canceled. When her mother returned home from Lutheran on November 22, she was feeling chipper, she wasn't the least bit disoriented, and she was perfectly pleasant to Claire. The Quintons would be going to Teaneck on November 25, Thanksgiving morning, as planned.

Jasmine came early on Thanksgiving morning to help Mrs. Quinton get washed and dressed. Barbara's daughter Sarah and her husband, Brian, came to fetch the Quintons at ten-twenty. They reached Teaneck at eleven-thirty. Sarah honked the horn on her car. Dwight came out. "Oh, you're here, Kate," he said. Twenty-five minutes later, he said to Claire, "Oh, by the way, happy Thanksgiving." Claire remembers being hurt by the slight. Sarah made sandwiches for lunch; Claire ate hers with a bottle of beer. Barbara had slipped ten days earlier and injured her ankle. Barbara's ankle was bandaged, and she could do only a limited amount of walking and standing. She politely told Dwight how to set the table, when to baste the turkey, and when to go to the florist to fetch the centerpiece for the table. She had prepared many of the vegetables and desserts ahead of time and had them in the freezer. Eleven people sat down to a Thanksgiving feast at the Gaylords' at 7 P.M. Barbara's cooking compared favorably with her mother's. After dinner, Claire lay down in the living room to rest her back. A while later, Mrs. Quinton went to bed. She slept on a convertible sofa in the living room.

Around eleven-forty-five, Barbara and Claire went into the family room to chat. Barbara was drinking Manhattans; Claire was drinking beer.

As Claire recalls the conversation, Barbara said, "I think Mama has a terrible 'I' problem."

"I just took her to the doctor a few weeks ago and got her new glasses," Claire said.

"I mean an 'I' problem — first-person-singular pronoun, as in 'I did this, I did that.'"

Barbara told Claire that her friend Helen Durbin had an awfully easy life. She had worked for a utility company for more than thirty years and would be getting a good pension. Claire knew that Helen had been having a hard time at work and a hard time at home with her sister, who was staying at her house while she was getting a divorce.

"Why don't you buy Helen's car?" Barbara asked.

"Helen's having a lot of trouble with her car, and there's nothing wrong with my Buick," Claire answered. "I had to put a new vinyl roof on it in April, but it's only got sixty thousand miles on it and it's running fine."

"Why don't you get a job as a civil servant?" Barbara asked.

"I don't think I could hack it," Claire said, and she reminded Barbara of a couple they both knew who had spent a life of misery in civil-service jobs. She thought of some of the grubby office buildings where civil servants worked in downtown Brooklyn. She didn't like to consider herself a snob, she said, but she had been accustomed to working for companies that had nicely decorated offices. Her bosses' offices had had carpeting, even if the area around her own desk hadn't.

"Claire, you never complain," Barbara said; she seemed to be on the verge of telling Claire to put their mother in a nursing home.

"What's the use of complaining?" Claire said.

Around one o'clock, Barbara said, "Let's pack it in."

Claire said she was going to check on her mother, read a little, have another bottle of beer, and go up to bed.

"Do you know how many beers you've had today?" Barbara asked. "Eight or nine."

"Yes, between one P.M. and one A.M.," Claire said.

Claire looked in on Mrs. Quinton and went upstairs to

bed. She hadn't been counting the Manhattans Barbara
had drunk during the day.

On Friday morning, Barbara shouted up to Claire's
room, "Rise and shine, it's Teaneck time." Claire brushed
her teeth, splashed some water on her face, and came
downstairs. "You'd better get rid of that commode," Barbara said. "I can't do it." Claire remembered that Barbara
had always hated changing her children's diapers. "When
did we go to bed last night?" Barbara asked.

"About one-fifteen," Claire answered, thinking to herself
that Barbara had criticized her beer drinking but that it
was Barbara who couldn't remember when they had
packed it in. Barbara had already helped her mother
from the sofa into her wheelchair. Claire emptied the
commode and helped her mother wash, dress, and do her
hair. Mrs. Quinton was wearing a red dress and a white
sweater. "Get that dress off your back," Barbara said
when she saw her mother in it. "It's too tight." Mrs.
Quinton weighed 110 pounds at the end of November.
The ten pounds she had gained — mostly from eating
butter cookies and ice cream during the afternoon — was
in her chest. "I realize it's too tight, but I'm wearing a
sweater over it and I'm not going to take it off," Mrs.
Quinton said.

On Friday evening, Barbara went to bed early. Claire
watched a heavyweight boxing match on TV with Dwight.
She tried to comment on the fight, but Dwight didn't
respond.

On Saturday, Kate and Claire Quinton were driven to
Sarah and Brian's house, which they had never seen.
Shortly after they returned to the Gaylords', they were

sent on their way. Barbara and Dwight were expecting twenty-two people for cocktails at five o'clock. Claire suspected that Barbara didn't want her guests to see her mother in her wheelchair, wearing molded shoes. Claire returned to Brooklyn considerably upset by the stay in Teaneck. She regarded Barbara as someone who put little sticks into people; the sticks were her gratuitous remarks, like the ones about Claire's beer drinking and her mother's dress.

On Monday, November 29, Kate Quinton told Jasmine that on Thursday evening, while Claire had been resting in the living room, she and Barbara and some of the other guests had been in the dining room. Barbara had said she wanted her mother's blue-and-white teapot; Mrs. Quinton told Jasmine she had lit into her older daughter. "I said to Barbara, 'Don't ever ask me for anything,'" Mrs. Quinton reported to Jasmine. "'If I want to give you anything, I'll give it and it will be from my heart. You have a sister, and someday she might want to use the teapot.'" Jasmine repeated the incident to Claire, who relished it. Her mother had given Barbara the fluted silver rosewater dish years before. Claire told her mother what Barbara had said about her "I" problem. "I probably shouldn't have done it, but if someone was coming at me with a knife I'd want to be forewarned," Claire told a friend.

⁊

One day in late November, Claire drove Jasmine to a food-stamp center. Other days, she gave Jasmine time off to go to the food-stamp center. Jasmine had had food stamps once before when Emilio was out of work. She had dutifully reported his return to work, and the food stamps had been discontinued. She told Claire she regretted her honesty. With Emilio on unemployment since spring, money was short. She said that when she went to reapply for food stamps she wouldn't tell anyone at the center that Emilio was collecting unemployment; she was going to say that he had taken off for the Caribbean. She told Claire that she planned to show the people at the food-stamp center her paycheck and to get a letter from her tenants saying that they paid only two hundred and some dollars rent a month instead of $350 — what they actually paid. Jasmine was awarded food stamps worth $231 a month. To express her gratitude to Claire for the ride and for the time off, she gave the Quintons a large bottle of ginger ale, a half gallon of milk, a package of corn muffins and one of bran muffins, a box of cookies, and two large packages of Philadelphia cream cheese. "Not a supermarket brand, a name brand," Claire observed. Mrs. Quinton had thought of applying for food stamps that fall after watching a segment of 60 Minutes which showed that people in Puerto Rico who were deemed eligible for food stamps were getting cash instead of food stamps and were spending the cash on many things besides food. "And they're not a state, they're just a commonwealth," Kate Quinton had said disparagingly.

After Jasmine had successfully reapplied for food stamps, Claire looked into the matter, learned that it would be advantageous for the Quintons to apply separately rather than together, and applied for food stamps first for her mother and then for herself. Kate Quinton had not been reluctant to go on Medicaid, as some other

T.C.P. patients have been. She felt she had worked hard all her life and hadn't asked the government for anything until she was almost eighty. When her Medicaid came through, she was delighted to learn that it was retroactive to January 1 and therefore she wouldn't have to pay Lutheran a $260 Medicare deductible for her January-to-March hospitalization. In 1981, she had had to pay Lutheran a $219 Medicare deductible when she was there for her breast operation. Medicare patients had to pay the full price for all prescriptions. Medicaid patients paid nothing for prescriptions. One of the main reasons her funds were always dwindling was her medical bills. She wanted to be sure to have enough money in the bank for a proper burial, which would cost about $4000. Kate Quinton was granted $75 a month in food stamps, Claire $17 a month. Claire soon found a store in the neighborhood that would accept the food stamps for cigarettes (her mother had resumed smoking a pack a day not long after the doctor advised her never to smoke again), paper towels and tissues, and other products for which food stamps were not supposed to be used. The Quintons also occasionally treated themselves to canned asparagus and other expensive groceries with their food stamps.

In December, Kate Quinton's arthritis became more painful. She rarely did her exercises or used her walker. She slept fitfully. At the same time, Claire came down with a bad cold. The Quintons were supposed to go to Teaneck for Christmas, but Claire couldn't face another holiday at the Gaylords'. She went to see a priest, described Thanksgiving in Teaneck, and told him that her mother's sisters had made plans to eat Christmas dinner together and that she had invited them to come to the apartment for dinner. She asked the priest if she had done wrong. He assured her that she had made a wise decision. The Quintons had a quietly festive Christmas dinner with Eileen and Sheila. Mrs. Quinton wrote two Christmas cards. She couldn't write any more, because of the arthritic pain in her right thumb and little finger. She couldn't even use her Bic lighter. Claire finished writing her mother's cards. Then she wrote her own cards, to some of her cousins and to several of the women she had worked with years ago on Wall Street, and mailed them on December 26.

Barbara and Dwight, Sarah and Brian, Elizabeth, Eileen, and two of Dwight's aunts came to the Quintons' on January 9, 1983, for a post-Christmas celebration. Barbara brought all the food, as well as plastic plates and utensils, and after a pleasant dinner she put all the plastic ware and paper ware into a trash bag she had brought with her and took it away, leaving the kitchen as tidy as it had been on her arrival. She and Dwight were flying to Arizona on February 1, and this was the last time the Quintons would see them before their departure. Dwight had bought time shares in a golf resort in Arizona several years before. The air-conditioning business was in its winter lull, and they were going to start looking for a retirement condominium. Claire was elated that Barbara and Dwight would be so far away.

Kate Quinton woke up on January 13 with a bad stomach ache. She went to the Family Physician clinic by ambulette. She had another urinary-tract infection. The rest of January was dreary. Mrs. Quinton didn't feel well.

Claire couldn't shake her cold, and spent a good deal of time in bed.

Friday, February 11, was Kate Quinton's eighty-first birthday. She received a number of telephone calls from friends and relatives. Charles and his wife, Jessica, telephoned from Arkansas, Barbara and Dwight from Arizona, and their daughter Elizabeth from Boston, where she was attending college. Eileen and Sheila had each sent a card and ten dollars. Barbara and Dwight had sent a card and twenty-five dollars, and Charles and Jessica had, too. Claire treated her mother to a shampoo and set by a visiting hairdresser and gave her a Mass card. Kate Quinton's birthday celebration was held a day late, because Brian, Sarah's husband, who was a computer operator, had had to go to night school on Friday. On the twelfth, he and Sarah brought assorted cold meats, salads, and bread for dinner, some cut flowers that Barbara had paid for, two pretty plants as their gift, and six balloons that were imprinted with "HAPPY BIRTHDAY GRANDMA." The two other guests were Janet Grafton, who brought Mrs. Quinton some hand lotion, and Helen Durbin, who brought her some cologne. Another family friend had given Mrs. Quinton a birthday cake. Claire put five candles on it — one for her mother, one each for Sarah and Brian, one for Janet Grafton, and one for Helen Durbin, all of whom had birthdays in February. When Kate Quinton was asked if she wanted a second piece of cake, she declined it, saying, "I have had an elegant sufficiency." The line was Claire's cue to say, "Any more would be a superfluous redundancy." A few days later, Claire took down the cards and the balloons. "There goes my birthday," Kate Quinton said wistfully.

Claire's cold dragged on into February. Some days, she couldn't keep her eyes open. Some days, she couldn't keep any food down. Jasmine made Claire tea and prepared muffins for her and did the grocery shopping. Claire's weight went down to 140 pounds; she was a size 12 again. On February 17, she woke up with a fever and couldn't eat. She telephoned Doctors-on-Call. The doctor who answered the call examined Claire. He prescribed an antibiotic for her cold and told her to take it for two weeks. He prescribed codeine for the pain she had in her chest as a result of months of coughing. On February 23, Claire was feeling no better. She called Family Physician Service. She was told to come to their clinic. She went there by car service with Jasmine late in the day, while a neighbor stayed with Mrs. Quinton. The doctor at the clinic took her temperature, listened to her heart, examined her stomach, and checked her lungs. He said they were clear, for which she was grateful: she had suffered from pleurisy several times in the past. He told her to take Tylenol. The following morning, Claire felt a little better; perhaps the two-and-a-half-month-long cold was breaking. She felt stronger. When Jasmine said "Kate, how about a walk?" her mother answered, "I don't feel up to it." Claire said, "Mama, you're going to do it." Kate Quinton walked slowly from the kitchen table to the kitchen sink and back to the table on the walker, with Jasmine behind her. It was only the third time in the new year that Mrs. Quinton had been on the walker, and her weak legs ached, but she said she was determined to regain the use of them.

February 24, 1983, was a cold day in New York City. Kate Quinton, a pale, thin elderly woman, sat in a wheelchair in her apartment in Brooklyn. While she and Jasmine Pagano, whom she had come to regard as highly as Mrs. Lawson had once regarded her, watched *Another World*, a few rays of sun illuminated the living room. By the time *Fantasy* was over, the sky had clouded and darkened. Snow had been predicted for the following day. Mrs. Quinton had never liked snow. At five o'clock, Kate Quinton sat in her kitchen sipping sherry and ginger ale. She listened to the ticktock of the grandfather clock she had first heard as a child in the kitchen of the house in Kirkintilloch. Time was passing as agreeably as she could expect. She looked forward to walking in the spring.

· ABOUT THE AUTHOR ·

Susan Sheehan is a writer on the staff of *The New Yorker*
and also the author of *Ten Vietnamese, A Welfare Mother,
A Prison and a Prisoner,* and *Is There No Place on Earth
for Me?,* for which she won a Pulitzer Prize. She lives in
Washington, D.C., with her husband, Neil, and their two
daughters.